An
Honorable Peace
in Central America

An
Honorable Peace
in Central America

Glen Caudill Dealy

Brooks/Cole Publishing Company
Pacific Grove, California

Brooks/Cole Publishing Company
A Division of Wadsworth, Inc.

Printed in the United States of America

10 9 8 7 6 5 4 3 2 1

Library of Congress Cataloging-in-Publication Data

Dealy, Glen Caudill.
    An honorable peace in Central America/by Glen Caudill Dealy.

    p. cm.
    Bibliography: p.
    Includes index.
    1. Central America—Foreign relations—United States. 2. United States—
Foreign relations—Central America. 3. Central America—Politics and
government—1979. 4. Representative government and representation—Central
America—History—20th century.   I. Title.
F1436.8.U6D43   1988   972.8'053—dc19   87-34489
ISBN 0-534-09312-4   CIP

The substance of article 1, "Can Non-Pluralist States Become Democracies,"
appeared in "Pipe Dream: The Pluralistic Latins," *Foreign Policy*, 57, Winter,
1984-85. Copyright 1984 by the Carnegie Endowment for International Peace.
An earlier version of article 2, "Is The United States A School For Central
America," appeared in *Virginia Quarterly Review*, 63(4), Autumn, 1987.

Sponsoring Editor: *Cynthia C. Stormer*
Marketing Representative: *Tamy Stenquist*
Editorial Assistant: *Mary Ann Zuzow*
Production Editor: *Linda Loba*
Manuscript Editor: *Barbara Kimmel*
Permissions Editor: *Carline Haga*
Interior and Cover Design: *Sharon L. Kinghan*
Typesetting: *Aldrich/Brown Consultants*
Printing and Binding: *Malloy Lithographing, Inc., Ann Arbor, MI*

To the memory of Bartolome de las Casas
(1474-1566) who heroically defended
Central Americans from the "benefit" of
aid packages sent by a great power that
could not distinguish between maintaining
its geopolitical hegemony and imposing
its ideology.

Preface

My friends here in Chile have known successively democracy, Marxism, and dictatorship; they also know the ambiguity of United States policy toward all three. In a recent discussion of U.S. foreign relations, conversation moved to an analysis of the American character. Finally the query came down to this: "Since individually U.S. citizens embrace those values, hopes, and promises symbolized by the Statue of Liberty, how is it that together they so often support causes, groups, and classes in Latin America that represent just the opposite?"

It is a good question. Although in a sense every page of this book is relevant to that issue, in a few paragraphs I would like to respond to it directly.

According to the international press, three American presidential candidates have already signaled their affinity for some kind of active intervention in Central America. From this distance their motives, while not clear, have a familiar ring. One notes that the Arias Peace Plan contains leftist ideas; another implies America has a religious duty to assist; and a third believes an invasion "would be welcomed by the people of Nicaragua." What these positions share with that of President Reagan and every former president at least since Eisenhower, is a strong American impulse to help others attain the kind of freedom and the form of government that we have known for 200 years.

This task seems altruistic and pure because when thinking about the Western Hemisphere, individual citizens as well as their leaders see no credible differences separating strategic priorities, other peoples' desires, and extending the American way of life. In fact, strictly speaking, since WW II the United States has had no foreign policy in Central America and the Caribbean; it has had a cultural policy.

However worthy in conception, "Americanism" leads to its antithesis for at least three reasons. First, because it does not link U. S. actions specifically to either national interest or Latin American realities, self-fulfilling myths must be created to meld together these ubiquitous factors. Since local peculiarities and distinctions south of the border have no standing within this model, dissenting groups and causes are condemned *a priori* as irrational or tools of outside forces. The bright light in New York's harbor is therefore in constant danger of being exchanged for Congressional arms appropriations.

Secondly, Americanism shifts the foreign policy focus to domestic politics, engendering competition among political contenders to convince the electorate that one course is more authentically "made in the U.S.A." than another. Once formulated in this language and forum, get tough rhetoric tied to our traditional ideals makes diplomacy sound weak-kneed and a compromise of principle. For example, President Carter's noble vision of a Latin America where human rights were protected put him on the side of the suffering masses; President Reagan's stress upon democratic rules and procedures inevitably aligns him with the oligarchs. Yet by themselves neither furnishes the basis for a workable agenda. By the end of his term, President Carter was caught between leftist representatives of those deprived masses and a U.S. electorate who wanted human rights but not communism. President Reagan's entire tenure could be characterized as grassroots support for democratic reforms in Central America, but not U.S.-sponsored oppression. As both these men stated their cause in the language of unnegotiable domestic values and historical apotheosis, diplomatic resolution was impossible.

Thirdly, Americanism fosters its opposite because it is inherently an "ethos of intention" unbounded by result. It turns a deaf ear to the truism—insistently taught by the late theologian Reinhold Niebuhr[*]—that moral cause can readily have immoral consequences. Foreign policy conceived by making carbon copies from a sacrosanct original master plate may be piously implemented, oblivious to possible deleterious effects. For example, few Chileans doubt that U.S. righteous encouragement and assistance to the anti-Allende, anti-Marxist forces, helped fuel murderous vengeance, torture, and general brutality during the early years of the Pinochet dictatorship.

Worse, the endeavor to press our form of government on others inherently impels us to abandon those principles that we set out to disseminate. The reason is evident: Liberal democracy rests upon the priority of local self-determination, a principle that is necessarily violated by every attempt to impose it from above or without.

Promoting human dignity in individual cases always redounds to our credit. But advancing a specific procedural course requires the United States to pass beyond the existential person to enter an alien and complex social-historical milieu where there will be winners and losers: *campesinos* face landowners, workers confront businessmen, the military clash with civilians, and the rich stare down the poor. By intervening to advance one group over another—each of which normally purports to favor democracy—we cease to be innocent advocates of principle and are transformed into a powerful factional participant in a contest whose consequences we cannot direct or foresee.

In short, it is *because* Americans are individually so susceptible to the discourse of principle that their collective contribution tends toward political repression. With moral cause and cloned governance having subsumed all other

---

[*] Reinhold Niebuhr, *Moral Man and Immoral Society* (New York: Scribner's, 1932).

variables, U.S. citizens feel naked and inefficacious before the threat of adversaries espousing different principles and different political forms, especially when these appear to be majoritarian movements. In such situations, local allies are too often found among the enemies of the people.

Foreign policy implies a concept of national goals, hopefully honorable, coupled with diplomatic initiatives to resolve antagonisms and find common ground. I believe if this country would have defined its policies in language devoid of Americanisms, a skillful diplomat like President Reagan's recent Special Envoy to Central America, Philip Habib, probably could have reached accord with the Sandinistas long ago.

Central America's immediate future will be determined by the August 1987 Peace Plan wherein leaders of these five countries dedicated themselves to collective problem solving. Their path is strewn with pitfalls: Dealing with rebelling groups may prove easier than harmonizing their own armed forces and privileged elites who have a mostly negative stake in fundamental reconciliation.

There may be pragmatic reasons for not endorsing this plan. But unfortunately when President Reagan decided to remain outside the discussions—until Nicaraguans have elections and become free—he sent an all too familiar coded message: Neither local self-determination nor negotiated quid pro quo will govern our behavior. Only the Americanization of Central America, their appropriation of our values and procedural mirror image, will be acceptable.

As long as that lodestar dominates U.S. policies, this country is unlikely to pursue a course that advances either Central American peace or North American honor.

Glen Caudill Dealy
Santiago, Chile
September 1987

Acknowledgments

It is a pleasure to acknowledge the assistance of others. Especially helpful comments, criticisms, and suggestions came from Ignacio Walker, William Appleman Williams, and Juan Gabriel Valdes. Useful observations on various parts of the manuscript were contributed by Beryl Crowe, Deborah Dealy-Browning, Rick Johnson, Gloria Levine, Bill Lunch, Ellen Morris, and Alan Tonelson.

I would also like to express my appreciation to reviewers of the manuscript for their interest and helpful critique: Professor Robert B. Anderson, Manchester College, Indiana; Professor Richard Baker, University of Oklahoma; Professor William Blough, Winthrop College, South Carolina; and Professor Daniel Levine, University of Michigan-Ann Arbor.

Carol Taaffe and Eliana Orrego Celis gave freely of their time along the way; Rob Sahr and Marolyn Welch resolved a multitude of computer mysteries.

Contents

An
Honorable Peace
in Central America

Introduction

Since President James Monroe, there has been domestic consensus that the U.S. geopolitical position mandates exclusion of foreign powers from Mexico, Central America, and the Caribbean, if not from all of Latin America. Our hemispheric policy has traditionally been crafted to achieve this objective.

The theme of these essays is that in recent times the United States has diverged from its customary course. Since 1954, *realpolitique* has become ambiguous and confused: Isolation of ideological regimes is often equated with the actual containment of our world antagonist. Indeed, probably at no time in the history of the Republic have strategic considerations of tangible foreign influence been more neglected or subordinated than under the anti-communist policy initiated by John Foster Dulles in Guatemala, continued most notably in the circumstances leading up to President John F. Kennedy's Bay of Pigs invasion, and persevered in by the Reagan administration's sponsorship of the *Contras*.

In a few words, by trying to destroy or quarantine Marxist/nationalist regimes for being heretical, rather than tolerating them as cases of internal populist realignment, the United States has opened a power vacuum that has literally invited the Russians into the area. The Cuban missile crisis can be characterized fairly as American resolve in the face of the Soviets testing the limits of that vacuum, not as a pragmatic policy of containment built on foresight. The *Contras*, established without a prayer of victory, ensured the militarization of the Sandinistas with Eastern Block assistance—the antithesis of containing foreign incursion.

In the Stalinist era of the Communist International—before the Russo-Chinese split and subsequent push by Russia's allies for their own cultural and nationalist identity—it may have made sense to fear ideological fellow-travelling as an automatic prelude to military alliance. It is now clear, however, that revolutions since World War II have not been sustained so much by the legitimacy and authority of their leftist doctrines as by their leaders' role in overthrowing imperial, or imperialist-allied, domination. Nationalism has proven to be the hypnotic catalyst.

The threat to U.S. interests in Central America is Russian might, not Marxist ideas. We have little to fear from nationalistic movements, however much to the Left they may be, as long as they do not align with Soviet power. Yet, our ongoing anti-communist policy increases the likelihood of that alliance. This is ironic because in the natural order of things, populist-based governments—including Marxist/nationalist orders—shun all foreigners. Nowhere have such regimes welcomed outsiders unless their territorial integrity was threatened. It is minority movements, like those of the Afghan Marxists or the Nicaraguan Somocistas, that encourage outside intervention in order to secure themselves against their own people.

Strategic interests require almost benign indifference toward those factors—tradition, political culture, ideology—over which U.S. diplomats have little control and the American polity can have little understanding. The Sandinistas, by virtue of their nationalist origins, are inherent antagonists of the United States. But they are also an expediential regime receptive to severing foreign military ties in exchange for their unqualified sovereignty. By accepting this reality, the United States could oust the Russians and eliminate the prevailing vacuum.

In the following essays I have tried to show why the anti-communist premises underlying our attempted subversion of first the Guatemalan Left, then Castro's Cuba, and now the Nicaraguan Sandinistas, do not stand scrutiny as a means for keeping the Russians at bay. Essentially, these assumptions fail because they emerged as countervailing dogmas to the Marxist challenge, rather than from a reasoned analysis of human desires and local political realities.

Our present policy has conjured up a universal man, teleologically driven toward liberal democracy. Capturing the heart and mind of this mythical being makes an ad hominem misreading of the Latin political ambience necessary. Specifically, we assume that Central Americans, as individuals, are longing for a kind of political freedom which the United States can bring; and that, as a whole, they embrace a political tradition similar to ours which only needs to be defended or reestablished in the area.

In denying these premises, the first two essays demonstrate America's lack of a solid prescriptive base for its current policy. Essay One proposes that Central American political culture is unitary, not pluralistic like our own, and therefore provides little foundation for U.S. assistance in building parallel democracies; Essay Two reveals that we have no idea how to satisfy populist demands in the area because our revolution was based upon freedom, while theirs are grounded in necessity. The third essay illustrates how the too facile merging of moralized anti-Marxism with U.S. self-interest, conspicuous in the politician's dread of being tagged as "soft on communism," has blinded our statesmen to geopolitical priorities.

A tough-minded alternative is found in seventeenth century Europe's *realpolitique*, which concluded an equally polarized era. Competing local princes had aligned with rival outside forces in the name of dogmatic truths. But contenders, adopting the slogan *Cuius Regio, Eius Religio* ("Whose the

Region, His the Religion"), eventually learned to coexist without incessantly reducing political and economic diversity to Protestant or Catholic differences and interests.

Political prudence suggests it is time for the United States to place its differences and interests vis-a-vis Central America in an equally pragmatic context. Living in a democratic age charged with nationalistic longings, we might accept the political reality inherent in the slogan, "Whom the Masses Sustain, Theirs the Refrain."

Can Nonpluralist States Become Democracies?

Since World War II the United States has reacted to real and imagined Soviet expansionism in Central America in the name of American-style pluralistic democracy. Liberals have urged Central American governments to guarantee human rights, hold free elections, and negotiate with their opponents in the best tradition of Western humanist government. Conservatives have provided arms in hopes of literally beating Marxist opposition into submission to give democratic forces a chance. Liberals and conservatives may differ substantially over the methods, but they agree on the desirability of pluralistic democracy and the belief that self-determination and democratic freedom are ultimately synonymous.

Currently the United States is working to build democracy in Central America on the assumption, as stated by President Ronald Reagan's former assistant secretary of state for inter-American affairs, Thomas Enders, that "only a genuinely pluralistic approach can enable a profoundly divided society to live with itself without violent convulsions."[1] This vision appears to be morally and politically unassailable. Overwhelmingly endorsed and seemingly beyond debate, it has made analysis of Central America's history, philosophy, and political experience appear irrelevant.

Yet except for Costa Rica, where a diverse immigrant population early formed a middle-class, property-owning society, the Latin American view is different. In Latin American minds the vision of freely competing factions all too often seems a choice between chaos and privilege. Latinos maintain that union comes from unity, not from diversity—*Ex unibus unum*, not *E pluribus unum*, has been and still is their motto. Their political beliefs are based on the corporatist medieval and Renaissance political theory that predated the contractarian thought of John Locke. The corporatists believe that society is best governed with some collective goal in mind. Latin Americans have always agreed with St. Thomas Aquinas that "it is the common good that unites the community."[2] Put in a twentieth century American idiom, what is good for General Motors is by definition bad for the country because, as Aquinas insists, "the particular interest and the common good are not identical."[3]

Thus Latin America's right-wing governments tend to conform to the type exemplified by former Nicaraguan dictator Anastasio Somoza Debayle. Left-wing regimes time and again stress the pluralism-unity theme of the Sandinistas who, in displacing Somoza, claimed that with the mass organizations they created of workers, peasants, and students "there is unity, but under revolutionary rule."[4] And centrist regimes, such as Mexico's *Partido Revolucionario Institucional* (PRI), pursue a goal similar to that of the Left by stressing—as has the U.S. Agency for International Development (AID) throughout Latin America—the importance of executive-level planning at the expense of any potentially faction-ridden, grassroots improvisation.

Unlike liberal democrats who believe that the general welfare unfolds and advances by protecting a large number of different groups, those both in and out of office in Central America agree that particularistic and opposing factions invariably disrupt public order and are insufficiently restrained by countervailing power centers.

For 175 years Latin American governments have endeavored not to balance competing centers of power, but either to expunge or to fuse them in the name of collective harmony. This enduring effort characterizes regimes both benign and arbitrary, civilian and military, rightist, leftist, or centrist. Coups and countercoups are familiar to most. But phenomena such as the Mexican one-party-dominated state, or the recent Colombian containment of conflict through periodic trading of the presidency between Liberals and Conservatives, also reflect a consistent drive for unified rulership. Viewed in that light, present-day Cuba presents only a late permutation of a long line of centralized governments. Its unitary aspirations are shared by regimes as diverse as those of Argentina, Bolivia, Guatemala, Panama, and

Paraguay. In a sense, Fidel Castro's left-wing dictatorship fulfills right-wing longings. As Argentina's semifascist dictator Juan Domingo Peron prophesied, "The society of the future will be a perfect harmony wherein no discordant note is heard."[5]

North Americans would like to believe that these endlessly centralized authoritarian regimes are just aberrations—perversions of the common person's fundamental desire for pluralistic government. But however superficially the constitutional orders of Latin American countries resemble those of the United States, they are ultimately grounded in Peron's premise.

These differences appeared with Latin American independence. That region's founding fathers held that only by way of an integrated, noncompetitive polity could thriving nations be created; they worried about their brothers to the north who were involved in an as yet unproved pluralistic experiment. Colombian Miguel Pombo's early nineteenth century preface to a Spanish translation of the U.S. Constitution goes to the heart of that concern:

> The more uniform character and customs of [Colombians] must create among them a more durable and close union than that established among the provinces of North America. The climate of these [North American colonies], their original formation, the different epochs in which they were founded by peoples that had diverse origin, diverse languages, different religion, different laws and customs, has formed . . . a heterogeneous body that with diverse necessities and diverse interests could not have that harmony that is so badly needed for the perfection of the general union.
>
> The uniformity of origin, language, religion, government, laws, and customs of the Provinces of Colombia must, on the contrary, tighten more easily the bonds of its reciprocal union, and establish on a solid basis a more perfect federation.[6]

The Latin American founding fathers accepted Jean Jacques Rousseau's premise that community flows from unanimity. Given a shared country of origin, Spanish Americans indeed had a great deal in common during their colonial past: one king, one system of law and administration, one religion, one military order, one language among their effective governing population, and one approach to education. Creating a political framework whereby that consensus might be continued seemed natural. This outlook was embraced by Simon Bolivar, political theorist to Spanish America, who criticized the tendency to borrow French and North American institutional forms. In a famous speech at Angostura, Colombia, in 1819, Bolivar rejected pluralist democracy, stating, "Unity, unity, unity must be our motto in all things. The blood of our citizens is varied: let it be mixed for the sake of unity. Our Constitution has divided the powers of government: let them be bound together to secure unity."[7]

Central Americans still pursue monolithic accord. Their fundamental laws seek, as the U.S. Constitution puts it, "to ensure domestic tranquility" not by establishing impersonal checks and balances but by encouraging governments to intervene actively on behalf of the community. The constitution of Guatemala, for example, reins in individuals and groups by stating, "The free exercise of the rights established by the Constitution is guaranteed with no limitations other than those deriving from the necessity of maintaining the public and social order."[8] From early nineteenth century military dictatorships throughout Latin America to contemporary death squads in Guatemala and the Marxist junta in Nicaragua, monolithic order has legitimated the neutralization of opposition groups. Thus Salvador Cayetano Carpio, the late Marxist leader of the Salvadoran popular liberation forces within El Salvador's Farabundo Marti National Liberation Front, articulated a long tradition when he said that "we have set out fully aware of what we are doing, with firm steps, on the road to the monolithic unity of all the people."[9]

Cayetano Carpio's holistic refrain recalls an earlier time. When the Spaniards temporarily regained control of Venezuela in 1812, Bolivar bitterly commented, "Party spirit determined everything and, consequently, caused us more disorganization than the circumstances themselves. Our division, not Spanish arms, returned us to slavery." Internal factions, "the fatal poison that laid the country in its tomb," had subverted the collective good.[10] Confronted with diversity, Bolivar sought unity by whatever means available. He decreed a *guerra a muerte:* Opponents, he said, "count on death, even though you are neutral."[11]

Few south of the border would disagree with Bolivar's historical diagnosis or his tough-minded response. Central Americans in particular, of every political stripe, reeling from their own version of a war to the death, today call for a similar total solution. The Right maintains that the choice is between communism and Christianity; the Left claims that it is between the oligarchy and the people; the Center has practically disappeared. Opponents are not acknowledged simply as representatives of other interests and ways of thinking, but rather are regarded as a menace to the community itself. And the community cannot be bartered, balanced, or negotiated. Diversity and anarchy are synonymous—evils to be removed together. Soon after overthrowing Marxist President Salvador Allende Gossens of Chile in 1973, General Augusto Pinochet Ugarte and his fellow officers thus began what leftist leader Miguel Enriquez termed "a war to the death, a war without prisoners" at the same time that they attempted to set up a new government whose participants would be nonpartisan.[12]

In the words of Bolivar—who, in 1814, it should be recalled, had more than 800 royalists taken from their dungeons and hospital beds and shot in cold blood in retribution for the brutality of his adversaries[13]—republics cannot be saved from chaos "unless [they] fuse the mass of the people, the government, the legislation, and the national spirit into a single united body."[14] Cuban President Fidel Castro echoed these sentiments when he observed that during the Cuban revolution, "the mass of our people understood the need for unity from the first moment and unity became an essential question for the revolution, unity became the cry of the masses, unity became a slogan of the whole people."[15] Bolivar and Castro demonstrate the continuing strength of a tradition that, if ignored, could cancel the effect of any good intentions by the United States.

      •   •   •

    Examples of Latin American ideals are found in two fundamental noncommunist revolutions of this century: Mexico under the PRI—which emerged in its current form in 1929—and Argentina under Peron during his initial period of rule from 1946 to 1955. The first of these is particularly instructive.

    True nationhood in Latin America began with the framing of the Mexican constitution at Queretaro in 1917. That event marked the beginning of an explicit adoption of nationalistic, centralized government throughout Central and South America after a disastrous, pseudopluralistic nineteenth century, born of an attempt to integrate the egalitarian-based contractual theories of the French and North American revolutions with the hierarchical and organic reality of Latin American culture. Everywhere the private had prevailed over the public. In the name of liberal constitutionalism's vaunted ideal of power sharing, the rich and the powerful dominated the poor, just as they do today in Central America.

    The Mexican Revolution broke away from this liberal facade, which was seen as responsible for most prior excesses, and returned to a traditional Roman Catholic ethical concern for the collective good. Interests of every kind—church, foreign, landed, and business—were battled by the revolution, and privileges were washed away in rivers of blood. Prerogatives were erased; social justice was reestablished as the rightful criterion for public action. A strong but relatively benign government was founded to rule in the name of the people. While elections were allowed, factious divisiveness was largely avoided by making each major interest group part of a corporate whole.

Since 1917, most countries in Latin America have at one time or another tried to emulate the Mexican model. In Cuba in 1940, for example, President Fulgencio Batista presented a constitution that in many respects mirrored the Mexican constitution of 1917. Batista's constitution provided for collective welfare with land reform and guarantees of work, shelter, clothing, and education. Castro's original promise, as outlined in his famous "History Will Absolve Me" speech of 1953, was to return Cuba to the principles of the constitution of 1940.

When Castro took power, most of his middle-class supporters soon felt betrayed by his sweeping reforms. They pointed to his earlier defense of the constitution and saw a contradiction. Yet the discrepancy was not in these principles per se. As surely as the Mexicans had done 40 years earlier, Castro, while embracing Marxism, engineered a social revolution by restoring a vision of the collective good that was implicit in the 1940 constitution but that was never implemented. And in his defense, the goals set forth in that document probably could not have been realized through the spurious liberal democracy favored by the privileged middle class. It was Castro who called Cubans to their colonial tradition of vox populi under the tutorial rule of the enlightened prince. The common good was and remains the stated referent of his policies: "There is only one interest," Castro has said, "the collective interest, the interest of all."[16]

A similar desire to recover their past and to escape from the perceived irrelevance of borrowed democratic structures now motivates reformers and revolutionaries in Central America. Nationalists believe that their first priority is to unify their peoples and provinces into a collective whole. U.S.

offers of pluralistic democracy do not advance this goal. One of the ironies of the present is that while the United States has made competitive democracy the cornerstone of its foreign policy, many Salvadorans and Guatemalans live in perpetual fear of death from numerous political factions, from the Left and from the Right. At the moment a pluralism gone mad is literally killing the *campesinos;* we tell them that it only needs to be tamed and constitutionalized.

For populations threatened by such violence, the appeal of communism—as well as of AID-sponsored cooperatives during the 1960s and 1970s—is grounded in the holistic, unitary nature of its vision. But the Mexican Revolution and the constitution that is so widely copied preceded the Bolshevik revolution. It is from Aquinas, Rousseau, and Auguste Comte, rather than from Marx and Lenin, that Central Americans ultimately derive their common political orientation. Nationalistic movements everywhere in the area attest more to a hoary agrarian desire for unity and justice provided by strong central government than to any new affinity for an alien ideology of middle-class property owners on the one hand, or dogmas of exploited industrial workers on the other.

While the United States attempts to foster pluralistic democracy in Central America, in reality it is perpetuating Central America's monolithic past. By exclusively supporting one faction, endorsing rigged elections, bribing the armed forces with materiel, and tacitly favoring exile or elimination of the opposition, America unwittingly advances state centralism. But that center can no longer hold because it excludes the interests of the *campesinos*, a majority on the move.

Latin Americans have a democratic tradition but not a pluralistic one. They embrace a pre-Lockeian view of popular sovereignty: The people may collectively overthrow an unjust prince, but for them to put effective checks upon his daily behavior or term in power is practically unheard of. Thus Latin Americans often speak of social democracy or economic democracy in which they envision a government of and for but not necessarily by the people. Human rights and elections, cornerstones of pluralistic government, take on new light when viewed within this context.

Human rights. The callous murder of nuns and AID contract workers in El Salvador a few years ago or the massacre of an entire hamlet of innocents in Guatemala leaves North Americans stunned. These events, however, should be seen within the larger framework of recent, government-sponsored torture in Argentina, Brazil, and Chile, and of the rough handling that undesirable political groups receive throughout Latin America. To put that violence in perspective, the civil war in Colombia during the 1940s and 1950s is estimated to have claimed 300,000 victims—more lives than the United States lost in all of World War II.[17] Whole village populations were raped, tortured, and slaughtered; individuals were murdered and sexually mutilated for no other reason than that they belonged to an opposing political party. In what has since come to be known as the *matanza*, the massacre, the military in tiny El Salvador slew more than 30,000 *campesinos* in 1932.[18] In Argentina between 1976 and 1980, an estimated 10,000 citizens lost their lives outright and 15,000 disappeared, often with a knock at the door in the middle of the night.[19] And so on.

While human rights in general are defended throughout the area, individual rights are not. Where political theory gives precedence to the common over the particular, individuals per se can hold no inalienable prerogatives. Collective ends inevitably limit liberty since personal freedom invariably conflicts with community goals. Aquinas, the official Church dogmatist, was precise in teaching Catholic culture this qualification: "Laws are passed to ensure the smooth running of the commonwealth. Unrestricted rights are not allowed in any civil constitution. Even in a democratic state, where the whole people exercise power, rights are not absolute but relative."[20]

Therefore, early Latin American thinkers and politicians not surprisingly reinterpreted Enlightenment premises in order to protect the community; the "Rights of Man" became "the common rights of men." If rights were common instead of individual, it seemed logical to name them and characterize them as collective goals to be sought rather than as freedoms to be protected; thus the list of social rights guaranteed by contemporary Central American constitutions and the popular tendency to associate freedom with bread, schools, and hospitals.

Neither philosophically, constitutionally, nor practically are persons to enjoy unabridged freedom of speech, assembly, petition, religion, or the protection afforded by habeas corpus; a bill of rights would deny public preeminence over private interests. From their Latin American point of view, regimes should disallow any individual autonomy contrary to the whole. Unlike the U.S. Constitution, which states that Congress shall make no law prohibiting or abridging one's rights, the constitution of Honduras typically guarantees the exercise of all religions "provided they do not violate the law and public policy"; provides for free expression but permits the law to "establish prior censorship to protect the ethical and cultural values of society"; and guarantees freedom of association "not contrary to public policy or to public morals."[21] Throughout Latin America, rights or privileges immune from constitutional curbs favoring the community are practically unknown. Hence, the 1950 Nicaraguan constitution, under which Somoza ruled, said, "The state guarantees individual liberty. It may not be restricted except in conformity with the laws."[22]

Criticism of rights violations is almost meaningless to Central American authorities since those who challenge their governance thereby oppose the collective will, which is normally defined as order. A regime that has won an election may feel that, as the community's authentic representative, it is even more justified in its barbarity; indeed, those who eliminate subversives might be honored rather than prosecuted. Consequently, until a show trial was put on for the United States, not a single Salvadoran army officer was disciplined for the thousands of murders and other human rights abuses there. And one of the alleged killers of two labor advisers was apparently rewarded with a red Ford Mustang, according to the *New York Times*.[23]

"The inability to deal with simple matters of justice in the face of crimes of this nature is inexcusable," declared Secretary of State George Shultz.[24] But that perception is unstudied; it assumes a functioning pluralistic democracy with the will and means to carry out "simple matters of justice." Shultz overlooks cause and cure of Central American strife. The cause is a concept of community that requires either the consolidation or the extermination of opposition. Given extensive pressure for inclusion of *campesino* interests, the oligarchs, with tacit U.S. assistance, have chosen extermination. But cure in Latin America has always come by allowing the ante to rise to a point where defenders of privilege are forced by self-interest to accommodate wider demands, as occurred after World War II when the middle class gained protection for its interests almost everywhere in Latin America. By arming the Right, the United States only delays that inevitable accommodation.

Elections. In general, Central Americans perceive constitutionally prescribed elections to be yet one more divisive threat to the community. By accenting differences, elections exacerbate latent conflicts and disrupt the whole both in theory and in practice. Partisan speeches, stuffed ballot boxes, extravagant claims of alternate teleologies, and military coups are just a few of the factors that have come to characterize the so-called electoral process. Little wonder that incumbents prefer to avoid such tumult as long as possible. One finds the same reticence to hold elections in Cuba and Marxist Nicaragua as in Guatemala or El Salvador—and for similar reasons.

Latin Americans consider guided elections necessary because the alternative—transferring power based on uninhibited voting—suggests a community without collective goals and a theory of equality, both of which they deny. During their infancies, Latin American states incorporated eighteenth century Spanish American conventional wisdom into their constitutions. As Bolivar said, "Nature makes men unequal in intelligence, temperament, strength, and character."[25] That view has formed the de facto, and only in a slightly qualified fashion, the de jure basis for government ever since.

Few question the inherent political inequality, since government based upon a preconceived end requires some unique individual or individuals to interpret that end. The theory of "one man, one vote" undercuts this notion by allowing numbers rather than wisdom to determine the direction of the whole. Moreover, Central Americans are persuaded that superior government comes from above rather than from the sagacity of numerous particular judgments. In personal experience during three years of teaching graduate students in Guatemala and Nicaragua, for example, there was never a single individual of any political orientation with an unqualified belief in the popular vote. While some, in fact, voted in order to avoid penalties—according to State Department figures, Guatemalans recently filed nearly as many blank ballots as they cast for the party that won the election—none saw an imperative for politicians to assume or surrender power merely because the people had spoken. "Should the community's welfare, the Rousseauian General Will, be neglected or annulled by coalitions of self-interest?" they would ask. "Do the majority poor know what is good for the country?" "Can students direct their teachers?" And philosophy aside, talking to an illiterate peasant in a Central American cornfield makes one realize questions of that nature have no self-evident answer.

Where monolithic aspirations provide a backdrop to political action, the ruling regime can reasonably promise elections either when it has a shaky hold on power, as in El Salvador, or when it has complete confidence in its ability to win, as in Nicaragua under both the Somoza and the Sandinista regimes. They are usually carried out, however, when a government so totally controls the political machinery that it has little chance of losing, as for example in Mexico, or is so disgraced and divided, as was the recent military government of Argentina, that it prudently gives up its position in order to regroup. Thus the electoral process often turns out to be a tactical move by military or civilian power brokers in the face of a diversity that they feel temporarily incapable of either integrating or eliminating; or alternatively, provides a symbolic plebiscitary affirmation of their rule.

Consequently, elections demonstrate neither faith in the intelligence of the people nor a desire to abide by their decision. Nor do they necessarily represent progress toward pluralistic democracy, as the United States apparently wants to believe. Because authority in Latin America gains its legitimacy from the ends it pursues, which makes it indivisible, power is rarely transferred peacefully through the ballot. But North Americans persist in thinking otherwise. The United States, for example, spent $2 million on the last Salvadoran presidential contest in an effort to make it tidy, honest, and efficient.

Yet Salvadorans have not lacked competitive democracy since 1823 because they have not known how to hold a technically fair election. Electoral victory may legitimate a regime in North American eyes—unless, of course, the Left wins as it did in Chile more than a decade ago and in Nicaragua in 1984—but for most Central Americans it is merely another form of elitist coup. To laud the processes of government by claiming that many Salvadorans had heroically "trudged for miles" to "vote for freedom,"[26] as President Reagan did in an April 1983 speech to Congress, creates the chimera of a foot-worn following as dedicated to democracy as Camel cigarette smokers to their brand. Such statements ignore the fact that the voting process from the ordinary person's viewpoint was unexceptional: There was no major opposition; there were statutory financial penalties for not voting; and one might be viewed as a rebel sympathizer for failing to cast a ballot.

American policymakers and their supporters have argued that military assistance is needed in Central America until new constitutions are written, elections held, trials conducted, legitimate government installed, and the Marxists defeated. This scenario, however, rests upon the illusion that impersonal rules can help a fragmenting political community. By hiding behind the facade of liberal democracy, an oligarchy can, through legalistic maneuvering and promises, gain respectability from the North while denying its own people the necessities of life.

. . .

Central American countries today are disintegrating from within. Americans have developed two major theories to explain why. "The contemporary forms of authoritarian domination are the direct or indirect result of the establishment of oligarchic republics during the bourgeois revolutions of 1870-1871," according to liberal academics such as Federico Gil, Enrique A. Baloyra, and Lars Schoultz. This "reactionary despotism" has deteriorated in Central America, the three authors explain, "due primarily to endogenous factors."[27] Conservatives, following Samuel Huntington's 1969 study *Political Order in Changing Societies,* argue that while traditional and modern societies can achieve political order, transitional polities, such as those of Central America, are characterized by instability, which opens the door to foreign intervention, violence, and guerrilla warfare.[28] Adherents of the first analysis typically propose as a cure promoting those local forces that, in the words of Gil, Baloyra, and Schoultz, are "trying to implement a process of democratic transition."[29] Partisans of the second school of thought emphasize checking external interference. But both theories unite in their teleological assumption, as stated in the *Report of the President's National Bipartisan Commission on Central America,* that the region "is in mid-passage from the predominantly authoritarian patterns of the past to . . . the predominantly democratic pluralism of the future."[30]

A less narrow-minded assessment would show that since independence, durable Central American regimes have held together a monolithic whole by paying attention to the corporate parts. On their own terms these political orders were relatively viable until World War II. But during the 1960s and 1970s the area went through its greatest period of growth and economic differentiation. As social differences increased and became more visible, tensions sharpened because the oligarchy was either unwilling or unable to accommodate new demands. Instead, in El Salvador, Guatemala, Honduras, and Nicaragua, governments reacted with repression. Guatemalan social scientist Edelberto Torres-Rivas points out that social protest then "tended to overflow the boundaries imposed by its corporatist origin, and rapidly took on a political dimension."[31] It has not been the failure of the liberal democratic constitutional patina that has brought these governments to their knees, but, as in pre-1910 Mexico, Batista's Cuba, and pre-1979 Nicaragua, the inability to include newly articulated social and economic interests within a political vision that had always rejected pluralism.

James Madison wrote in *The Federalist* that it was "vain to say that enlightened statesmen will be able to adjust . . . clashing interests."[32] America's founding fathers put their faith in law and system. Latin Americans, by contrast, decided with Bolivar that "codes, systems, statutes, wise as they may be, are useless works having but small influence on societies: virtuous men, patriotic men, learned men make republics."[33]   Accordingly, they placed their trust in the shrewdness of an enlightened ruler.   Like a Renaissance prince, such an individual is supposed to personify prudence and to mold his regime "to the nature of the circumstances, the times, and the men that comprise it," as Bolivar stated.   If prosperity and peace reign, he continued, "the government should be mild and protecting; but if . . . turbulence and disaster [prevail], it should be stern and arm itself with a firmness that matches the dangers, without regard for laws or constitutions until happiness and peace have been reestablished."[34]

This vision corresponds with Central American practice.   Minimal peace and individual security have coincided with the consolidation of control in individual hands.   Congress and courts operate—often constitutionally—not to contain or neutralize an executive's might, but as instruments of his tutorial rule.   Such extraordinary power is sometimes used for worthy ends, as it was by Guatemala's great nineteenth century liberal statesman Justo Rufino Barrios; frequently the legacy is more ambiguous, as exemplified by Guatemala's early twentieth century law-and-order caudillo Jorge Ubico. But certainly without that dominance things fall apart, as in the current case of El Salvador.   The Salvadoran military's impudent disregard for presidential orders, coupled with a U.S. attempt to shore up a nonexistent pluralistic democracy, have brought near disaster and a partitioning of the country into Left and Right sectors.

The United States simplistically describes the crisis in Central America as a struggle between democratically oriented individuals and communists.   Yet the chaotic political situation is more reminiscent of sixteenth century Italy, as J. H. Plumb's description of the period in his *The Italian Renaissance* suggests:

> War was constant.   And not only war—so was treason, murder, and plot, for this reason.   Some states lacked con-

stitutions, they were without the constitutional formalization of social, economic, and political power that was sanctioned by tradition or by law. Power was captured by groups, by interrelated families, sometimes depending on oligarchic, sometimes on popular, support, and occasionally on the help of other city-states and, in time, on foreign invasion. Exiles from all states abounded, to become the instruments of aggression: murder, trickery, and civil war were accepted elements of political activity.[35]

The United States proposes to apply the magical "heals every wound" potion of a pluralistic democracy derived from Locke's social contract theories to this harsh environment, and speaks of due process, free elections, human rights, and separation of power. Yet for most Central Americans who consider procedural checks and guarantees to be merely tools of the reigning despot, Niccolo Machiavelli's *The Prince* offers more appropriate means for ending the turmoil.

Latin American regimes committed to centralization eventually face a legitimacy test that divides them into one of two types: those that endeavor to rule in the name of the whole by integrating diverse interests—such as civilian-led Mexico, Panama under the late populist President Omar Torrijos Herrera, and Marxist Nicaragua—and those that aim to govern in the name of a privileged part of that whole by excluding or, if need be, eliminating representatives of the less privileged, as happened in Guatemala and El Salvador. The masses consider the first type of government legitimate but not the second.

Chile and Uruguay, each seen as a showcase of democracy for half a century, demonstrate the weakness of procedural democracies that fail this legitimacy test. Hit with economic crises, both governments collapsed when their elected leaders were perceived as partial and unable to exert sufficient personal dominance over the society to integrate corporate interests into a collective whole. The military junta that overthrew Allende, charging that his government "had broken national unity," said, "The President of the Republic has demonstrated to the country that his personal power is conditioned upon the decisions of committees and executives of political parties and groups which associate with him, thus losing the image of maximum authority which the Constitution assigns him, and therefore the presidential character of the Government."[36]

In practice, legitimacy is won or lost mostly by the chief executive. Successful caudillo politics requires the common man to believe, as in medieval and Renaissance times, that the prince is ready to protect him and the community at large from a predatory, privileged minority of landowning barons and commercial entrepreneurs. In turn, viable rule demands the leader's recognition that his position and tenure rest upon a populist base. As Machiavelli noted, "it is necessary for a prince to possess the friendship of the people; otherwise he has no recourse in times of adversity."[37]

This explains the ultimate failure of so many Latin American presidents whose power is rooted in class prerogative and U.S. weaponry. The dictatorships of Batista, Castro, Pinochet, Somoza, and Rafael Trujillo Molina of the Dominican Republic were workable only as long as they were perceived to be friends of the people. However, when economically and militarily dominant governments, like Pinochet's regime, become partial and elitist, their days are numbered. The general population, having little stake in the survival of such orders, remains on the sidelines as innocents. Opinion shifts almost completely to the Left, which has consciously taken up every popular cause.

Wherever located on the political spectrum, Latin American regimes tend to survive as long as their populist base holds. This phenomenon has little to do with ideology, as demonstrated by the contrasting legacies of Peron, who was groomed in fascist Italy, and Castro. Even General Pinochet understands that truth and is today travelling his country initiating housing projects, telling Chileans how lucky they are to know law and order, patronizing diverse local causes.

The lesson seems apparent: The United States could profitably de-emphasize inapplicable democratic procedures in favor of support for friendly, non-Marxist leaders with real or potential mass appeal. However ideologically unpalatable this proposal is, America should reconsider its focus on electoral legitimacy and heed the words of Torrijos when he gently chided Senator Edward Kennedy (D.-Massachusetts) in 1972. Kennedy, he said, had fallen into "the generalized error of North American politicians of classifying Latin American governments by their origins and not by their intentions."[38]

The United States might also review its avowed emphasis on adjudication to promote human rights. Leaders should be judged by their orientation with respect to the collective whole rather than by their defense of individual rights per se. Only the former carries weight within that heritage. Strong men are scorned not for employing coercion but for using it to attain particularistic ends. If generals and their death squads' bestial means divide rather than unite the polity, they can effectively be called to account within that framework. U.S. foreign policy would benefit enormously from adopting—particularly in Central America—the method that Latin Americans have used since colonial times to distinguish between good and bad regimes. Good rulers are those who practice what might be called an economy of violence,[39] not those who protect every individual right.

     •   •   •

In her frequently cited essay "Dictatorships and Double Standards," in the November 1979 issue of *Commentary*, then Georgetown University professor Jeane Kirkpatrick called Torrijos "a swaggering Latin dictator of Castroite bent."[40] But he is more accurately seen as almost the archetypal good Central American leader, one that the United States could support to its advantage. Unquestionably Machiavellian, he came to power in a coup. Enjoying a strong power base in the National Guard, he engaged in an ongoing balancing act, juggling students, bankers, U.S. politicians, Panama Canal workers, multinational corporations, and Marxists. He aided the anti-Somoza forces in Nicaragua, called Castro his friend, and courted U.S. economic aid; he was corrupt, tried to ban political opposition, wrote his own constitution, and had himself designated "Maximum Leader of the Panamanian Revolution." Yet this grand caudillo deserved American approval.

In his commencement speech at Harvard University in 1983, the Mexican novelist Carlos Fuentes commented that "before becoming a democracy, Mexico first had to become a nation."[41] After years of fragmentation, injustice, and strife, El Salvador, Guatemala, Honduras, Nicaragua, and Panama during the early 1970s needed leaders who could overcome their respective multiple dichotomies to form a nation. Torrijos filled the void for Panama, as the Sandinistas have done in Nicaragua. He became the Great Protector, which necessarily meant that he denounced exploitation in all its forms—including that often unrestrained economic opportunism practiced by foreign and local entrepreneurs alike. He integrated the large rural population, theretofore ignored, into national life and became a hero to the common person with his many projects and trips throughout the countryside.

Like medieval sovereigns, Latin American caudillos can become known as "good kings" by stopping flagrant, systematic abuses of power. Little in the way of concrete social action is required. Not raising bus fares can be more significant to poor people than promises of future benefits. Torrijos' success as a national integrator allowed benign rule and vice versa: His helicopter visits were greeted with cheers rather than fear.

Central American countries, like Mexico's one-party-dominant state, are not now and may never become democratic in the American sense of the word. The question is whether individuals will arise to fulfill the terms of their own political heritage. Can they end the degenerative pluralization of the whole? Will they, like Torrijos, reinterpret and broaden their ideology of collective well-being to encompass those who live on the margin of society? Or will they leave that task to Marxist caudillos?

The United States may pour millions into Central America to strengthen pluralistic democracy in order to legitimate governments, but if Washington ignores integrating leaders or popular movements it will probably come up empty-handed. A procedural fortress provides a weak barrier against the Marxist Left. And as Machiavelli wrote to his prince, "When once the people have taken arms against you, there will never be lacking foreigners to assist them."[42]

While assertions of pluralistic democracy—such as U.S. Ambassador Thomas Pickering's March 1, 1984, statement that "El Salvador aspires to and clearly is entitled to the kind of government to which we also believe we are entitled"[43]—unquestionably assure ordinary Americans that the United States is taking the moral high road, in practice these views cannot help but prolong the human and material devastation of the area. Central Americans consider it axiomatic that the judicial, electoral, and administrative processes are only as fair as the regime in power.

"That government is best which governs least" may be a sensible dictum for liberal democracy. In Central America, as in Renaissance Italy, laissez-faire regimes have neither precedent nor utility. Governments either rule in the name of the whole or are eventually overthrown regardless of their electoral origins. Allende's Chile demonstrated that the Left is no more immune to that principle than the Right. America's heavy reliance upon an image of pluralistic government effectively places its national security interests on a political vision outside the range of Central American philosophical and pragmatic possibility.

Is the United States a School for Central America?

Americans, like ancient Athenians, are proud people who believe their form of government worthy of universal emulation. "We are the school of Hellas," boasted Pericles in his famous oration, and today the United States would like to think itself a school for the Americas. To the extent the non-pluralist character of Latin institutions and culture is understood in this country, it has been greeted as challenge rather than barrier. Like obstinate children whom we placed in a slow-learners class 175 years ago, the ever patient teacher would correct such deviant unitary tendencies with good will (aid)—or discipline (intervention).

Conveying U.S. style democracy to Central Americans has been a high priority for both the Carter and Reagan administrations. President Carter sought to school Latin America in the individual's right to due process. The Reagan administration began its tenure calling that human rights policy utopian, because "it measured all countries by the same standards—disregarding differences in history, political traditions and social conditions."[1] However, the President soon appointed a "school board," The National Bipartisan Commission on Central America, made up primarily of amateurs in the region's cultural inheritance, language and politics, to gauge the chances for implementing his own 1776 vision of freedom and democracy. Successively, each administration had set out with diplomacy and appropriations to fulfill its particular version of U.S. "higher law."

Superimposing interpretations of the American creed upon Central America's discredited democratic past and intolerable present, Carter and Reagan policies coincide in their insistence that nationalistic movements attempt the impossible—that they be legitimate within the framework of our own political tradition.

That tradition in fact provides no solution to the key difficulties facing these nations. Indeed, Central America fits George F. Kennan's startling observation that "we have nothing to teach the world. We have to confess that we have not got the answers to the problems of human society in the modern age."[2] Those sentiments, perhaps overstated and certainly rejected by the American people, rest upon the irrefutable uniqueness of our national experience.

America's higher law, far from offering a plan of deliverance to the Central American masses, stands dumbfounded before an unfree people in a state of deprivation. Rooted in eighteenth century "laws of nature and of nature's God," our War of Independence was fought for individual rights in particular and political freedom in general, rather than to solve everyman's socioeconomic difficulties. Our founders singularly devoted their lives and fortunes to political liberty because there were no urgent needs, no suffering nor abject poverty requiring them "to submit to necessity, no pity to lead them astray from reason."[3] Yet, Americans and their spokesmen, with Patrick Henry's voice ringing in their ears, now say, in effect, "even though most of you citizens of Guatemala, El Salvador, Honduras, Nicaragua and Panama are poor, illiterate, sick, own no property and have no experience in local town councils, if your revolutions are about life's necessities rather than about political liberty and pluralist democracy, they are not legitimate."

Paradigms of political freedom derived from a revolution whose participants had already fulfilled their basic economic wants are rationally neglected as irrelevant, or dismissed as inadequate, by the Central American masses and their representatives. However ideologically valid, leaders who speak of concrete remedies for the uncertainties of everyday life reasonably gain a more attentive audience. Nicolas Berdyaev recounted this peasant realism at the time of Russia's 1917 Revolution. In *The Origin of Russian Communism*, he wrote, "the old government had lost all moral authority; people had no faith in it. . . . Liberal ideas, ideas of right as well as ideas of social reform, appeared, in Russia, to be utopian." In this ambience, Marxism, with its attention to peace, land, and bread, "showed itself to be much less utopian and much more realist, much more in accord with the whole complex situation in Russia in 1917."[4]

Justifiably proud of our message, in practice the United States' procedural "fix" of popular elections and due process is tied to a reality Central Americans have never known—respect for individual opinions, interests, and rights. These appear idealistic and unfeasible before their preoccupation with security and well-being—a still to be attained assurance that from the lowered vigilance of sleep they will awaken to tranquility, tortillas, and beans, rather than to machine-gun fire or hunger. Our diplomats largely sidestep such tangible fears and desires by simply assuming that morally superior political philosophy, like one's religion, carries its own legitimizing papers, and that only leaders of good will are wanting in order to win the hearts and minds of the masses.

But that is not so. "The great political ideologies of the past which captured the imagination of men and moved them to political action . . . were successful not because they were true," wrote Hans Morgenthau, "but because they gave the people to whom they appealed what they were waiting for both in terms of knowledge and in terms of action."[5] Peoples of Central America are demonstrably unwilling to fight for any political theory or structural arrangement that does not promise them deliverance from misery. The Salvadoran's and Nicaraguan's attention—and this includes CIA paid *Contras*—is primarily upon short and long term routes to improved personal welfare and security. It may be an unwelcome truth, but, as Hannah Arendt concluded from her analysis of revolutions, "liberation from necessity, because of its urgency, will always take precedence over the building of freedom."[6]

Central Americans have historically shown themselves to be less motivated to replace self-imposed leaders with electorally legitimized alternatives than, depending upon class status, to either abrogate or defend an inherently unjust order of existence. Consequently, self-limitations necessary for reasonable dialogue readily give way to the boundless violence of oppressor and oppressed. President Napoleon Duarte's failure to reach a successful agreement with his guerrilla opponents is a foregone conclusion because the latter are as dedicated to altering the nature of El Salvador's fourteen family control as El Salvador's military-civilian oligarchy is dedicated, however indirectly, to preserving it. The situation is reversed in Guatemala, but the conclusion must be similar: Vinicio Cerezo, the populist candidate allowed to take power through the grace of a few generals, will be unable to negotiate fruitfully with the military-oligarchic alliance whose very existence is threatened by his proposed integration of the Maya-Quiche Indian majority into the political life of the nation. It is within this context that U.S. insistence upon the government of Daniel Ortega holding meaningful reconciliation talks with the *Contras* should be understood as futile.[7]

America's higher law ideology of political freedom not only furnishes no feasible guidelines to these three nationalistic presidents of good will, but indeed runs counter to the logic of the conditions which they face. Its Newtonian vision of autonomous parts contractually coming together in pluralist government or open marketplace ignores the imperative for collective action on behalf of a dispossessed poor; what Barrington Moore, Jr. has termed the "unity of misery and the diversity of happiness."[8] As such, U.S. diplomacy speaks in incomprehensible syllables of liberty rather than of necessity. This contradiction would have emerged long ago had not theory been denied in practice by providing massive aid to endangered regimes and movements we favor. Indeed, the one positive areawide program haltingly advanced by this administration, the Jackson Plan, which would have implemented the economic assistance provisions of the Kissinger Report (a recommended $1.2 billion for fiscal 1987) foresaw political freedom built upon local well-being. Unfortunately, that liberty involves the ambiguous legacy of discontinuous

Congressional appropriations and continuous misappropriation by recipient officials. (Somoza's downfall was due in no small part to the Nicaraguan business sector's withdrawal of support after he channeled millions of Agency for International Development funds for earthquake relief into his own enterprises.)

      ·   ·   ·

American democracy's language of individual freedom is reasoned self-interest; Central America's language of personal necessity is compassion. American democracy's protection for collective freedom is the multiplicity of interests; Central America's solution to collective necessity is the unity of interests, nationalism.

It is futile to teach our higher law, a variant of Plato's abstract "truth by the discourse of reason,"[9] to individuals in search of compassion; thinkers from Plato to Maslow have recognized the priority of physiological need over political self-actualization. The United States in Central America is attempting a political solution to a social and economic question in which concepts of freedom and public action are perceived to be largely irrelevant. Nicaragua's citizens, some of the poorest in this hemisphere, pragmatically placed little faith in Somoza's legal-rational prescription for poverty relief through a corrupted capitalism's "hidden hand" that seemed to reward those who were already affluent; but they line up with hope before personalized benefactors like Interior Minister Tomas Borge who, working in a building adorned with a sign announcing the "Sentinel of the People's Happiness,"[10] opens his door once a week to any petitioner.

Liberal democracy, the government of reasonable forms and rational processes, found its model in a text crafted for a people of abundance ("in the beginning all the world was America"); who enjoyed absolute liberty ("a state of perfect freedom to order their actions and dispose of their possessions and persons as they think fit"); followed a God who rewarded effort (He "gave the world" to the use of the "industrious and rational"); and were guided by a natural law ("and reason . . . is that law").[11] These phrases from *The Second Treatise on Civil Government* by John Locke appealed to a citizenry that already had peace, land, and bread for the taking. (It is worth recalling that Locke wrote an essay on "The Reason-ableness of Christianity" that could be illuminatingly juxta-posed to compassion-oriented tracts in Liberation Theology, which center upon Christ's reading from the book of the prophet Isaiah: "The Spirit of the Lord is upon me, because he has anointed me to preach the gospel to the poor . . . to set at liberty those who are oppressed.")[12]

Such reason-oriented government grounded in a vision of equal and autonomous contracting persons sounds coun-terfeit to individuals living in a poor, hierarchically based, socioreligious order of haves and have-nots. Locke's belief that "reason . . . teaches all mankind who will consult it, that, being all equal and independent, no one ought to harm another in his life, health, liberty, or possessions," and that "there can-not be supposed any such subordination among us, that may authorize us to destroy one another, as if we were made for one another's uses,"[13] is contrary to Central American his-tory, everyday experience, and, I would suggest, "reason-able" expectations in the foreseeable future.

Difficult though their task of creating a workable gov-ernment may have been, our constitutional fathers were not saddled with the simultaneous foundation of political order and provision for man's fundamental social and physical needs. Under that dual burden every modern revolution since 1789 has succumbed to the priority of human necessity, and initially established some form of nonplural, nonfree central-ized state. However evil such regimes may appear to outsid-ers (Nicaragua's vice president, Sergio Ramirez, said in 1984, "the literacy campaign is a priority. The improvement of the health system is a priority. Housing is a priority. Organizing an electoral system is not a priority of the government ")[14], it should be understood that this centralization of power has not only been welcomed, but demanded by suffering masses whose experience of man's prepolitical state, contrary to Locke's vision and our ancestor's reality, has been one of scarcity, irrational allocations, and limited freedom. There has been little land for use by the "industrious," and cooperative efforts have been rewarded as often with violent death as with affluent security.

While our founders sought little more than to remedy politically an obvious defect of an abundant frontier—protection for one's property—much more drives Central Americans. Middle-class Cubans and Nicaraguans who fled to Miami, accusing revolutionary leaderships in their swing to the Left of reneging on democratic promises, omit the fact that these movements were driven to that position not only by sinister Marxist-Leninist cabals, but by a popular cry for nearly everything except political liberty. Movements born in scarcity readily abandon freedom as an expendable luxury. "Of all ideas and sentiments which prepared the [French] Revolution," noted Tocqueville, "the notion and the taste of public liberty, strictly speaking, were the first to disappear."[15]

And those new regimes, despite their broad economic failures, undeniably have produced compassion: twenty-five years after toppling the old order, Cubans have "a life expectancy of seventy-three years, an infant mortality rate of 17 per 1,000 live births, a literacy rate of 96 percent, per capita income of $1,417."[16] While comparable statistics for Nicaragua seven years after the revolution are incomplete and suspect, in part because data from the Somoza era were so patently imaginary, experts agree that dramatic gains have been accomplished in these same categories—many now nullified by the war effort.

For a people focused upon everyday needs, it also means much to know that their leaders, however authoritarian, probably have no Swiss bank accounts. From the common man's point of view, to return to electoral competition could expose the revolution to the danger of reactionary minorities: reminders of the Batista and Somoza dictatorships where, for their ruler's gain and glory, the individual's vote was uncounted and his life was discounted.

Although outstripping the old "democracies" in fulfilling basic necessities, the Marxist/nationalist governments of Cuba and Nicaragua have unfortunately not addressed the realm of political freedom. They naively maintain that liberty will flow from a dialectical resolution of class antagonisms, the end of exploitation, and a more just distribution of goods. Marxist regimes everywhere demonstrate that Hegel erred in believing freedom would evolve according to historical imperatives without conscious human action. Yet their partisans are undoubtedly correct in holding that socioeconomic liberation has everywhere been a condition of political freedom (although by no means does it lead automatically to it).[17]

Just now, seventy years after their revolution confronted "the social question" in a sanguinary struggle, Mexicans are beginning to demand pluralistic rights and political competition to solve staggering problems. The original promise has not been fulfilled. But, in undergoing an ultimately integrating national revolution, Mexico founded an order embued with authority—the source of law and the origin of power—and government assumed the obligation to deal with necessity. This combination of popularly bestowed authority and accepted political responsibility has provided successive Mexican regimes with a presumption of legitimacy and stability, and Mexicans with a relatively open society. By contrast, when assuaging biological needs is beyond the concern of ruling oligarchies as in Guatemala, where "the private sector does not seem to want to assume any responsibility . . . for developing the infrastructure or the well-being of the population as a whole,"[18] one can hardly fault the rationality of hard-pressed *campesinos* in heeding the siren song of nationalist deliverers.

Collective necessity calls forth nationalism. It is not differentiation and multiplicity, but nationalistic unity that offers hope to distressed individuals. Every Central American populist movement is sustained by the promise of collective freedom from an oppressive existence attributed to local or foreign power arrogation operating contrary to the common welfare. Leaders and their suffering followers are uninterested in replicating nineteenth century pluralistic divide-and-rule minority governments that left them impoverished. In common with citizens of Algeria and Vietnam, neither "democratism" nor communism, but nationalism is the credo for which the masses have demonstrated a willingness to risk their lives. Movements are built around national heroes (Marti, Sandino, Farabundo Marti); adopt national titles [the Sandinista National Liberation Front, the Farabundo Marti National Liberation Front (El Salvador), the Guatemalan National Revolutionary Unity]; and proclaim nationalist slogans ["Patria libre o morir" (Nicaragua), "Patria o muerte! Venceremos!" (Cuba)].

Nationalism in Latin America presents itself as liberation from outside forces. That is the attracting message of nonrevolutionary regimes as diverse as Peron's Argentina, Stroessner's Paraguay, and Garcia's Peru. ("Alan Garcia has been elected by 20 million Peruvians and not by international bank officials. Peru has one overwhelming creditor: it is our own people."[19]) Think then of the energy and exaltation loosed by the 1979 popular uprising in Nicaragua that visibly ejected overlordship! "People felt for the first time as if they were the bosses in their own country. It was a country that had always before been someone else's—it wasn't our country, it was almost like a foreign country," said Tomas Borge.[20] In this euphoria it does little good to warn of future totalitarianism or the heresy of their saviors. Franklin Roosevelt is alleged to have remarked that "Somoza may be a son-of-a-bitch, but he is our son-of-a-bitch." Surely Americans are sophisticated enough to understand that Cubans and Nicaraguans now rejoice in saying the same of Castro and Ortega.

Our higher law background envisioning individual freedom stands uncomfortable, mute before political figures who speak of freedom in a nationalist context. Guatemala's populist president, Cerezo Arevalo, spoke the truth when he observed, "the Americans don't like people with very nationalistic sentiments."[21] We fear and oppose nationalism inasmuch as, unlike our own drive for personal liberty which was illegal but accommodated within the law, elsewhere freedom from necessity has seen the very laws themselves displaced. During the French Revolution, St. Just chillingly remarked that all "is permitted to those who act in the revolutionary direction."[22] His statement speaks to a situation where a privileged sector rules with no intention of self-destructing and, legally or illegally, means to protect that position. Such sentiments bring terror to our hearts when expressed from the proximity of Central America because we intuit the chasmic gulf between any shade of government rooted in the legitimacy of the past (i.e., its laws and constitutions), and a populist movement searching for validation in truths, inevitably abstract, proclaiming a future order where justice will reign.

Central American constitutional polities, such as that of El Salvador, were founded with minimal popular consent and are ultimately maintained through violence. Citizens there never formed a social contract, however fictitious, either among themselves or with their leaders; constitutions were not submitted to the electorate for debate and ratification. Lacking historical and psychic approval, without fundamental authority and empowerment by the people, such regimes must rely upon ever heightened coercion to sustain control over populations that increasingly resent their misery. Within this context of illegitimacy, albeit veiled by electoral and legalistic rituals, governments inevitably turn to outside sources for weapons of internal coercion; force is substituted for learning, school is turned into barracks.

Meanwhile, the deprived masses easily embrace Rousseau's *union sacree*, fount of Robespierre's "despotism of liberty." Grounded in Catholic unitary philosophy of the common good, Latin Americans have always been lukewarm toward a separation and division of powers. Dissatisfied citizens readily adopt one-party premises common to both the French Revolution and to Marxism. "The people" form a collective relationship with their advocates to oppose the existing "despotism of interests." In the current revolutionary situation, unanimity is rewarded and prepares a climate whereby "we," a self-righteous nationalist majority, face "them," counterrevolutionaries and enemies of the people who, in the name of pluralist privilege, support a system unresponsive to the demands of poverty.

From the point of view of American higher law, both right and left participants in the contest are usurpers of individual freedom. Thus, U.S. policymakers offer up status quo arguments, frightened scholastic distinctions between authoritarian evil and totalitarian evil, which merely obscure and detract from the great fear engendered by a people remaking themselves under any lawless label, let alone one associated with our world antagonist. Fear has not, however, filled our minds with tolerance or humility toward a populist revolutionary situation before which we stand powerful, but speechless. Resorting to moralistic ideology, smugly contending all nations are traveling on our inexorable freedom course, we leave unstudied the differences and difficulties of every particular quest, a people's unique history and culture, their words, deeds, and immediate aspirations.

•   •   •

In the fourth century B.C., Thucydides wrote, "as long as poverty gives men the courage of necessity . . . so long will the impulse never be wanting to drive men into danger."[23] Latin American *campesinos* increasingly demonstrate a willingness to forfeit usually evanescent political freedoms for tangible alleviation of suffering. Given the concrete personal motives of those majorities, nothing could be more certain than the eventual areawide success of national liberation movements.

Although these masses are no more intellectually attracted to Lenin than to Locke—twenty-five years after the Revolution Cubans still show little curiosity about Marxism—from the late General Torrijos on the Right, to Cerezo and Duarte in the Center, to Ortega and Castro on the Left, to the guerrillas in the mountains, populist leaders have all used categories and concepts of collective struggle. Quite naturally, any theory offering an explanation for the cause of their woes or suggesting a justifiable solution, gains a hearing and advocates. Communism and Liberation Theology provide both, and it is not by chance that the governing directorate in Managua includes priests and Marxists.

Arrogance of power and righteousness of conviction blind us to the irrelevance of words and armaments unattuned to popular needs. Our founding fathers, more steeped in political philosophy than recent statesmen, were less sanguine about the possibilities for the accommodation of republican government in countries of vastly different size and circumstance. Correct or not in their conclusions, these men at least appreciated the uniqueness of their situation. Skeptical of using the Greek city-state as a pattern for the United States, they suggest the complexity in extending representative government to Central American sized nations. A small polity, said Madison, "can admit of no cure from the mischiefs of faction. . . . Such democracies have ever been spectacles of turbulence and contention; have ever been found incompatible with personal security, or the rights of property; and have, in general, been as short in their lives, as they have been violent in their deaths."[24]

During the Spanish-American War, William Graham Sumner warned, if this nation "attempts to be school-mistress to others, it will shrivel up into the same vanity and self-conceit of which Spain now presents an example."[25] Establishing the internal justice of another nation living another agenda is not Anglo-Saxon man's burden and historically, short of cultural and physical annexation, such instruction has not been carried to a happy conclusion.

"Whom the Masses Sustain, Theirs the Refrain"

In his *History of the Peloponnesian War*, Thucydides (b. 460 B.C.), Greek general and historian, recounts a countryman's advice on the proper stance toward a small state that had treacherously joined Sparta, Athens' authoritarian enemy: "The question before us as sensible men is not their guilt, but our interests. . . . The question is not justice, but how to make them useful to Athens."[1]

The United States, confirmed in its dedication to schooling Central America, has lost sight of that distinction. Political prudence has been sacrificed on an altar to moral-strategic symmetry. As Elliott Abrams, assistant secretary of state for inter-American affairs, has repeatedly declared, "in Nicaragua our moral goals and our security interests are identical";[2] or as The National Bipartisan Commission on Central America maintained, "this is one of those instances in which the requirements of national interest and the commands of conscience coincide."[3]

An assumed unity of conscience and interest, of morality and power, has blinded us to the nature of the threat posed by the Sandinistas, and to pragmatic remedies. Goals have become cloudy. How sharply focused upon national security is an approach which avows "the struggle (in Nicaragua) is not right versus left, but right versus wrong," as President Reagan contends;[4] or one which portrays the United States as a righteous polity that cannot "walk away from one of the greatest moral challenges in postwar history"?[5] Strategic thinking is no longer keenly honed when the secretary of state's rationale for *Contra* aid is our "moral duty" to prevent Nicaragua from falling into "the endless darkness of communist tyranny."[6] *Realpolitique* suddenly sounds like a nineteenth century missionary society debating the fate of blackest Africa, or Cortes contemplating the liberation of Aztecs from their non-Christian leaders.

Our moralistic stance is the historical prelude to holy war—Calvin's presumption to plead the cause of all the godly.[7] Merging self-interest with virtue, life-threatening designs have been attributed to the iniquitous Sandinistas that appear to leave Americans a stark choice between using force to exorcise evil, or to suffer individual destruction through ungodly or unpatriotic inaction. President Reagan, like Hobbes, would enroll government as the instrument for man's deliverance from private fears of violent death. The president plays upon our dread of personal dissolution to gain support for containing communism: If the red horde is not now forcibly deterred in Nicaragua, one day "they" will be outside "your" door.

Most of our allies are incredulous before that scenario. How, they ask, can the world's greatest military power be preoccupied with a squalid little republic of 2.9 million inhabitants? To which many Americans, tutored in postwar political theology, respond in anxious terms regarding the dangers of "where-do-we-stop-them?" communism.

Our dread has been misappropriated. The tangible danger of personal destruction by Soviet missiles has been speciously aligned with a psychic fear of harm at the hands of ideologically inspired millions pawing at the gates of Texas. George F. Kennan's original formulation of containment policy wisely said nothing about checking the spread of discordant ideas: It is Soviet power, not Marxism or Nicaraguans, that can break our bones.[8] A misplaced focus has sent us on a crusade into Central America to counter Marxist/nationalist movements with sponsored democratic governments out of the conviction that the requirements of national interest and the commands of conscience coincide. To secure our bodies, we have been called not simply to act upon geopolitical realities, but to check the growth of a heretical creed.

This contemporary intertwining of moralistic democracy with strategic interests—an extension of American democracy's missionary role as envisioned by Woodrow Wilson who, ironically, has been villified by conservative "realists" ever since—was initiated when, challenged by

Soviet postwar expansionist tendencies, the United States reacted not to an actual Russian presence in Central America, but to the ideological leanings of populist leaders. Secretary of State John Foster Dulles, using American power and influence to defeat Guatemalan Leftists in 1954, inaugurated an anti-communist policy which, unlike previous moralistic interventions principally directed toward protecting or advancing perceptible economic interests, would require far-reaching intrusion into these nation's social and political structures. Dulles ignored Kennan's doctrine of containing tangible Russian power for the quixotic task of checking Marxist ideologues.

To win this crusade for the constancy of our neighbors, it appeared necessary to use force, and America's pietistic tradition has been able to find justification in violence when the cause is sufficiently sacred. (It could have been Torquemada, but it was Luther who helped fuel Europe's Wars of Religion, instructing the prince that when "your entire land is in peril . . . it is a Christian act and an act of love confidently to kill, rob, and pillage the enemy, and to do anything that can injure him until one has conquered him according to the methods of war."[9]) Thus, while every American citizen today can be appalled at Rigoberta Menchu's description of Guatemalan army forces torturing her 14-year-old brother—"they ripped off his fingernails, cut off his tongue, they destroyed the soles of his feet and burned his skin"[10]—probably a majority give at least tacit consent to the current administration's annual request for funding that army because our anti-communist cause seems so ultimately justified, even if this particular Indian boy were innocent of everything except joining a cooperative.

      •   •   •

The United States finds itself on the well-trod path of other imperial powers that have tried to maintain or extend their suzerainty over rebellious, but relatively weak, peoples.

The benefactor arrives with political-economic-religious truths believed to be sown in the heart of man, which, if accepted, would almost guarantee the lesser nation's place within the greater nation's sphere of influence; these dogmas are resisted by the potential recipient as a pretext for conquest or control. Finally, the rejected benefactory power concludes that given the validity of its principles, it can in good conscience "force them to be free."

Latin America's indigenous populations first suffered beneficence at the service of universal truth 500 years ago when Spanish troops stormed ashore putting to the sword all who refused to acknowledge Divine Right of the one true God and his imperial messenger, the King of Spain. They received ideological invaders a second time when a band of emissaries landed at the Bay of Pigs, archetypes called forth by U.S. post-1954 reunification of its moral and strategic priorities. Forerunners of the *Contras*, they were bringing democratic "higher law" to a Marxist/nationalist pagan order. Each group of intruders, miniscule in relation to the numbers due for proselytization, arrived confident that natives would respond to the veracity and justice of their cause. When that did not happen, when many recalcitrants were discovered opposed first to Soldiers of the Cross, and subsequently, to Soldiers of Democracy, the message-carrying power remained undaunted, righteous in its conviction that peoples everywhere could resist such truth only out of ignorance or false consciousness. Consequently, disaffected local chieftains were sought, however ungodly or undemocratic, to become rewarded proxies in a great enterprise to force hesitant subjects to opt initially for Christianity, and later, for "freedom."

Conquering the New World under a Christianizing banner required the Spanish monarchy to rescue indigenous Americans from evil; the conquistadors read a proclamation to the obstinate natives saying, "if you do not acknowledge this (Christian faith) . . . or if you maliciously delay in doing so, I declare unto you that with God's help I shall advance upon you with fire and sword and I shall make war upon you everywhere and in every way I can."[11] A human rights oriented sector of the Spanish clergy protested so effectively that King Charles V ordered the machinery of conquest to cease until a more just policy toward the natives could be ascertained.

Justice seemed to require that if native Latin Americans were, like Europeans, capable of deciding the validity of the Christian message, they could not be brutally subdued. Thus, in 1550 a debate was held at Valladolid, Spain, "on whether, according to Aristotle, Indians were rational men or natural slaves?" Contending theologians and counselors did not question the need to convert the populace to Spain's inclusive political-religious ideology; as with contemporary American consensus on the benefits of pluralist democracy, "no Spaniard doubted the Indians' need of the Christian message."[12] At issue was its delivery. Should natives first be instructed in the Christian faith, or should they be overpowered in a just war and thereby made receptive?

Spawned by a sense of altruism and the desire to maintain strategic dominance, the United States is indirectly undergoing a similar self-exhortatory debate on how to deliver democracy to Central Americans: Should they be schooled by oligarchic proxies, forcibly quelled and made amenable by "freedom fighters," or possibly defeated by Marines? Were the inquiry focused it would ask, "Is democratic freedom sown in the hearts and minds of Central Americans?" and if so, "Does that innate impulse legitimize a just war to save them from Marxist heresy?"

The confident American response to the question of human nature is found not in Aristotle but in a Bible-interpreted Declaration of Independence: "Freedom is not the sole prerogative of a chosen few," says President Reagan citing conventional wisdom, "it is the universal right of all God's children."[13] That assertion magically metamorphizes the intrusion of U.S. power into Nicaragua from an act of imperial domination, or defense against Soviet expansionism, into a missionary-like expediting of a people's self-determination.

Regardless of man's inherent biological orientation toward political freedom, however, such a justification for foreign intervention is as culture-bound and self-interested as the Spanish crown's prior subjugation of Latin America. Forced by the Valladolid debates to acknowledge that Indians were rational and did possess souls, the monarchy determined that continued paternal action was necessary to guide them out of a savage state toward realization of their own true selves. Just so, our foreign policy determinists are currently unwilling to let the alleged democratic impulse take its natural course without American direction.

At the turn of the century, the United States practiced unabashed religious justification for incursions into the decaying Spanish empire. Surely future historians will see in our present Central American policy a venture open to the kind of skepticism called up by President McKinley's often cited midnight conversion initiating the Spanish-American War (1898), which gave the Philippines and Cuba to the United States. Falling on his knees, he tells us, he "prayed Almighty God for light and guidance," and arose convinced of a compassionate duty to intervene in order "to educate the Filipinos, and uplift and civilize and Christianize them, and by God's grace to do the very best we could by them, as our fellowmen for whom Christ also died."[14]

Today we seek to democratize rather than to Christianize. The terminology is one of freeing instead of civilizing, and scriptural correlates are sought in social science paradigms peppered with eschatologically charged democracy-at-the-end-of-time precepts such as "developing nations," "modernization," or "governments in transition," but the parallel is clear: A self-evident infallible end legitimizes almost any means, however contrary to our own sense of domestic political morality. An ideologically grounded view of human destiny has transformed every Central American into a latent democrat awaiting redemptive assistance.

Genetic, or destinarian, democracy as the source of a reactionary Central American policy was first defended in Milton Eisenhower's report to his brother in the aftermath of that administration's foray into Guatemala's internal affairs. "Most peoples want freedom," he said, "though many have never experienced it." Equating freedom with democracy, Eisenhower arrived at the conclusion, advanced by Machiavelli in *Il Discorsi*, that it is possible for a dictatorial agent to found a government of free men: "By cooperating with them (the people), even through dictators—by keeping open the lines of communication—one may hope that a growing understanding of the strength, glory, and basic morality of democracy will enable the people of a harshly ruled country to achieve and maintain democratic institutions of their own design."[15] Intervention on behalf of an authoritarian rightwing regime had become an ennobling task to effect a popular change of conscience; i.e., to actualize what already existed within everyman's inner self. Central Americans acquired a new tutor bringing democracy for their souls and subjection to their bodies; the United States began to recapitulate Spanish colonialism which had "lovingly propelled them toward heaven by blows."[16]

Since the Eisenhower presidency, regimes and commandos armed with correct democratic ideology have repeatedly been sent on an "errand into the wilderness"—to borrow Perry Miller's descriptive phrase for Puritan New Englander's religious-political mission—to restrain citizens who, against their true nature, appear in danger of naively responding to revolutionary socialist promises.[17] As the common man innately wills his own freedom, but does not recognize the poisoned character of leftist antichrists who would deceptively lead him to tyranny, self-appointed agents of the community are justified in acting upon Rousseau's tough-minded dictum, "who wills the end, wills also the means."[18] The CIA's *Nicaragua Manual* explains: "whenever it is necessary to use armed force in an occupation or visit to a town," *Contras* (therein designated "Christian guerrillas"), should "admit frankly and publicly . . . that this action, although it is not desirable, is necessary because the final objective of the insurrection is a free and democratic society, where acts of force are not necessary."[19]

Violence against a people in order to assist their authentic selves and save them from enslavement, whether carried out by fellow citizens or a foreign power, is now considered not only legitimate but humanitarian. Though a stranger to the blessings of liberty, a Central American innocent killed with democratic intent serves higher law. Unjustly tortured or shot by American trained troops of an anti-communist rebel group or military dictatorship—no doubt promising a purifying election in the near future—he does not give up his life in vain since, as Rousseau bluntly put it, "when the prince says to him (the subject), 'It is expedient, in the interests of the State, that you should die,' die he must."[20]

•   •   •

"A democracy is incapable of empire," wrote Thucydides. You want to believe your policies abroad reflect your principles at home, "entirely forgetting that your empire is a despotism and your subjects disaffected conspirators, whose obedience is insured . . . by your own strength, and not their loyalty."[21] In Eastern Europe and Afghanistan the Soviets have found that pursuing national security through ideologically aligned buffer states has made them the Colossus of the East for the same reasons that the United States is seen as the Colossus of the North in this hemisphere. It provides little solace to divert the point with protestations against moral equivalency; the bottom line is that on Russia's western flank and the United States' southern flank an elite, oriented toward and benefitting from a dominant power, holds a nationalistic majority at bay. The significant difference is that Russia's imperialism is an extension of her internal colonialism, while American imperialism is contrary to her own most cherished values.

Refusing to acknowledge that a republican form of government was historically translated into the Central American setting without substance, that excepting Costa Rica the few have habitually controlled the many, we persist in thinking that national interest is served by supporting predaceous "democracies." Determined to teach good citizenship, the United States injudiciously chooses its pupils from among the Central American upper middle classes and the oligarchs, those who have a vested interest not in learning limitations upon power, but in retaining the status quo of their exclusivity. We attempt to tutor these political brokers in the legal niceties of protecting human rights, professionalizing the military, and computerizing elections—as if their domestic problems were quintessentially technical—and leave the *demos*, that majority who are ill-housed, ill-clothed, and ill-fed, to proselytizing solutions offered by our nondemocratic antagonists on the political Left.

Asserting the unity of morality and power, America ignores one of the oldest distinctions of political philosophy: Right constitutions or regimes are focused upon the interests of a whole community, wrong constitutions or regimes are concerned with the particular interests of rulers (Aristotle).[22] The natural order of allies has been reversed. Contrary to the Peloponnesian War which saw the Hellenic world convulsed, "struggles being everywhere made by the popular chiefs to bring in the (democratic) Athenians, and by the oligarchs to introduce the (nondemocratic) Spartans,"[23] Central America's oligarchic minority plead for, and obtain, economic assistance from a democratic United States in order to gain their distance from the masses, and military arms to protect that separation.

Our democratic rhetoric, intent upon capturing the common man's heart and mind, ignores his prepolitical Hobbesian desire for freedom from the fear of violent death on the one hand, and freedom from want on the other. In despair, popular chiefs turn to Marxist justifications for their role as spokesmen of the many; and to Cuba and the Soviet Union for weapons, as an antidote to U.S. economic aid and armaments in support of the few.

Continued assistance to oligarchies in Honduras, Guatemala, and El Salvador where generals have final say despite elected heads of state; victory for the CIA-created and supplied *Contras* based in Honduras; a Marine landing and inevitable establishment of a Somoza-type puppet capable of containing the Left in Nicaragua or El Salvador; each would leave the many at the direction of the few. By fostering and maintaining a privileged, exploitative, anti-communist elite who control the symbols and processes of freedom, and by villifying as antithetical to democratic government every populist/nationalist/Marxist movement of the poor majority who resist such exploitation, the United States has worked itself into a theoretical corner from which, in practice, *nothing it does can have a desirable outcome.*

Under these conditions, U.S. policy can develop in three ways: (1) invade and hold the area for an extended period under the big power rationale that, as Thucydides said, "the strong do what they can and the weak suffer what they must";[24] (2) continue to aid paternalistic military despotisms that practice anti-communist genocide in the name of democratic freedom; or (3) consider the possibility that from the perspective of national interest rather than ideological purity, "soft on communism" might be a prudential policy.

The first alternative needs no comment because domestic politics precludes blatant long-term imperialism; the second is daily miring us deeper in the Central American quagmire. I shall discuss the third.

*   *   *

Keeping foreign powers at bay, the hemispheric goal set forth by President Monroe, has been American policy for over one and one-half centuries. (Secretary of State Richard Olney's contention in 1895 that the United States is "practically sovereign on this continent, and its fiat is law upon the subjects to which it confines its interposition,"[25] may have been wishful and certainly was imperialistic, but it had the merit of reflecting a great power's ambition, free from delusions of benevolent intent.) That perennial concern now calls the United States to focus upon Russian power. Containing and diminishing the Soviet presence in Cuba and Nicaragua is surely *the* priority of any reasonable Caribbean and Central American policy.

Our leaders, however, persist in domestically attuned ideological toughness to the neglect of pragmatic decisions and actions that could achieve this goal. Cowed by the unthinkable political dread—partly conjured by the lessons of China 35 years ago—of incurring responsibility for "losing" Central America through treating with the apostates, neither Republicans nor Democrats have had the courage to advocate guarantees for Nicaraguan national sovereignty in return for a greatly lessened Soviet presence. The Sandinistas have always been willing to acknowledge America's hegemony in exchange for a recognition of their right to exist. Everyone in the region expects the United States to continue being a powerful shark among lesser sardines, as Guatemala's first populist president Juan Jose Arevalo said;[26] or as a popular Panamanian song declares, "the war fish [shark] goes on swimming around the dominion that he rules." (El peje guerrero va pasando recorriendo el reino que domina.)

Mutual self-interest drives the United States and Nicaragua toward entente. For us, it would curb Russian influence, as occurred in Mexico during the 1930s where (contrary to U.S. fear of growing Marxist inroads) a nationalist one-party regime cut off all foreign intrusions from the Left. For Nicaraguans and other Central Americans, it would allow them to demilitarize and begin to respond to consumer wants.

The alternative to accepting Central American self-determination is a continued holy war attitude toward the region in an endeavor to align our pious ideological motives with our national interest. History suggests that, when the power and ambition of participants is shrouded in such righteousness, violence escalates without resolving the divisive issues.

The spurious Peace of Augsburg (1555), which presaged Europe's religious wars, is instructive. Under its terms, each state of the old Holy Roman Empire was permitted to be either Protestant or Catholic according to its leadership: *cuius regio, eius religio,* "whose the region, his the religion."[27] Many Europeans thought they couldn't live with the loss of ideologically correct states and provinces to wicked heretics. Thus began bloodshed, the Wars of Religion, which lasted one hundred years and ceased with The Peace of Westphalia (1648). By that time, what was unclear at the beginning had become evident to all: Moral principles dividing Protestants and Catholics were hopelessly intertwined with political interests, national security, and expansionism, as well as economic need and greed. *Cuius regio, eius religio* was belatedly accepted; but it was hardly a vindication or refutation of the commands of conscience. Time and the anguish of war had brought political realism.

A prudent Central American policy, taking account of the current dissolution of world communism into nationalistic units—reminiscent of Europe's fragmentation toward the end of the Wars of Religion—would embrace populist movements and regimes without fear. As the history of the West since the treaty of Westphalia shows, ideological persuasion exerts minimal influence over political alliances when strategic concerns are at stake. (Argentine generals allegedly tried to purchase missiles from the Soviets during the Falklands War; and those communists to whom we "lost" China in 1949, are now gaining Western nuclear technology through capitalist self-interested entente.)

We live within a democracy, natural ally of majoritarian movements and regimes. By definition, most citizens rejoice that their government is incapable of empire, but share that concern for national security inherent to peoples everywhere. Americans long for a policy that would reconcile local self-determination with U.S. hemispheric hegemony. And that practical amalgamation, negating every domestic what if debate over Sandinista motives and intentions, lies within our own hands.

The wisdom of Thucydides and the lesson of previous holy wars counsel the United States to unilaterally enunciate for Central American regimes the populist version of *cuius regio, eius religio:* "Whom the Masses Sustain, Theirs the Refrain." We would remove ourselves from the demeaning support of one form of tyrannical government as antidote to another. By accepting populist governments, the United States would give Central American oligarchs a compelling incentive to come to terms with legitimate *campesino*-based demands. That failing, nationalist movements, whether from Left, Right, or Center, could vie with one another in the knowledge that, however appalled Americans might be before Marxist slogans denying every higher law principle which we hold dear, the United States would not intrude unless, through misguided alliance with our enemy, our security were jeopardized. These countries would no longer find total mobilization to be in their interests. Like Mexico, they would have little inclination to create an extensive Russian presence, and consolidated support for Leftist leadership, consistently based upon anti-American nationalism, would inevitably erode.

Self-determination would not license Central Americans to interfere in their neighbors' affairs any more than it would permit the United States to intervene in Nicaragua's. As de facto guarantor of national integrity in the area, a non-proxied U.S. response to any regime that threatened its neighbors or acquired offensive weapons capable of reaching these shores would be supported by a majority of the American people who have consistently favored the Sandinistas' right to exist, but have also, when faced with tangible danger, as in the Cuban missile crisis, demonstrated single-minded support for the principle of nonintervention by outside powers.

Soft on local "isms," uncompromisingly tough toward Soviet power, acknowledging Central Americans' right to swim in the same ocean—albeit respectfully—these would serve our interests and our honor.

Is Pluralist Democracy on the Ascent in Latin America?

An anonymous reviewer of this manuscript challenges the contention that most Latin Americans do not embrace pluralistic democracy. It is denied, he says, by events outside Central America: "Argentina, Uruguay, and Brazil have recently returned to democratic rule in the midst of an outpouring of popular euphoria. This public exaltation (most vividly displayed in the huge demonstrations supporting Argentina's President Alfonsin against the military) certainly fails to support the author's claim of some long-standing cultural inheritance at odds with democratic values. Moreover, the large quantity of survey evidence collected in Latin America during the last thirty years shows widespread popular support for democracy."

This is an important critique since it is the major point upon which Americans can agree. From C. Wright Mills' *Listen Yankee* of the sixties to today's U.S. volunteer groups in Nicaragua, liberals have wanted to believe that a Latin America unoppressed by the United States or local strongmen would be a democratic Latin America. Conservatives, from President Eisenhower's Secretary of State John Foster Dulles to President Reagan and current state department spokesmen, have time and again maintained that a Latin America free of communism is essentially a democratic Latin America.

These coinciding conclusions have merit to the extent their partisans are speaking of Latin American variants of democracy. Unfortunately, both liberals and conservatives in this country rush to the assumption that once free of oppression, Latin American government would resemble our own pluralist model.

The fallacy of that position underlies 175 years of U.S. frustration. Whenever an open election is held south of the border and a populist candidate emerges, North Americans breath a sigh of relief thinking that good has finally triumphed over evil. One more nation has adopted our political paradigm. A few years or months later, we hear alarming news: There has been a coup d'etat, civil liberties have been abolished, individuals are being tortured, and the media is censored. We become depressed.

While it would be foolish for anyone to prophesy the future of another country based on past example, it is safe to say that culture informs political life everywhere in the world; that, as Berdyaev showed, twentieth century Soviet authoritarianism is an extension of nineteenth century Tsarist authoritarianism; or as is obvious, American democracy owes much to prior experiments in New England and "Old England." In other words, a people's orientation does not change from moment to moment but extends back into time and prepares the future.

Latin America has known other historic swings between liberty and despotism. Every society has various themes and facets, any one of which may be politically emphasized. For example, current Republican foreign policy focuses upon procedural democracy and laissez-faire economics; Democrats stress human rights. Each, however, are aspects of our tradition: both assume individual equality, limitation upon power, and political party competition.

The question today becomes, Has the liberty that Latin American peoples have periodically known been the freedom of pluralistic democracy or, like Mexico, that of an open society within an essentially monolithic political order? Are those exalting Argentine masses applauding the emergence of institutionalized diversity, or the victory of freedom and a populist hero after years of military suppression?

Surely Latin Americans love democracy, understood as an open society and freedom from every deprivation, as much as any peoples in the world. The mistake is to equate that affinity with a drive for pluralistic government. Three hundred years of centralized Spanish colonial rule and a Catholic hierarchical world view were melded during the independence era into the promise of the French and American Revolutions. But in this case, however liberal sounding, a unitary structural emphasis was maintained.[1]

Latin Americans have their own distinguished tradition of democracy. The qualifying adjective, however, is not pluralist but populist. That unitary tradition, sketched in Essay One, with roots in medieval conceptions of popular sovereignty, has in the modern age sometimes been characterized by liberty, for example Chile before 1964; sometimes by authoritarianism, for example Argentina under Peron; but hardly ever by pluralism.

The desire for freedom is like the desire for wealth. As Max Weber demonstrated in his introduction to *The Protestant Ethic and the Spirit of Capitalism* everyone wants to be rich; the question becomes, which peoples possess those rational virtues contributive toward that end? A poll taken anywhere in Latin America would no doubt show overwhelming support for a democratic order. But does that mean a commitment to either the type of democracy we enjoy or to the rational means essential for that governance—a people culturally disposed to uphold minority rights, shun violence, seek pragmatic (nonideological) solutions, preserve a loyal opposition, and favor compromises even when one's party holds absolute power?

In August 1987, Carlos Huneeus Madge published *Los Chilenos y la Politica,* based upon survey research data. He found in this land of repressive military dictatorship, that "democracy is the political order desired by the great majority of Chilenos"; 70% according to his poll.[2] What does that imply? If the forces of oppression were toppled, could one realistically suppose a pluralistic environment would automatically reign as North Americans want to believe?

What will occur is a moot point until events overtake theorizing, but perspective can be gained by asking how Chile, called a showcase of democracy for half a century, became an authoritarian order.

In "Cultura y Democracia: Una Mirada desde la Clase Politica," political scientist Juan Gabriel Valdes writes of an attitude that has pervaded Chilean life of the recent past and present: "A vision which assigns to politics the primordial sense of an activity whose objective is to implant a particular truth in society; a truth which stems from rational knowledge." Who opposes that truth "exhibits deliberate irrationality or expresses interests contrary to historical necessity."[3]

In the 1960s, says Valdes, the Christian Democrats became the center party. Although they had no authoritarian designs, the more pragmatic politics of previous years was diminished: "Christian Democracy represented a cultivated and modern center, but at the same time, it introduced into the political scene, the logic of a party of ideas, of a party constituted around a truth which makes all its members carriers of that idea." As this attitude escalates across the political spectrum, "each actor exacerbates the exclusive profile of his proposal; each partial advance is decreed insufficient; each decision or measure in the economic, social or political area, can be disqualified in the face of a theoretical model, a moral imperative for all those adhering to it."[4] The Left, participating in that vision of a unitary raison d'etat, helped elect Marxist President Salvador Allende. Chaos eventually ensued, the military intervened—and continued the vision.

After the military coup, the Right "was brought together by a group of intellectuals to embark upon the most extreme ideological adventure in the country's history. The so called Chicago model became in fact the most feverish point of ideological inflation initiated in Chile during the decade of the 1960s. The attempt was to impose a model of society based on an individualistic ethos—the 'new man' of capitalism—which would cancel politics in exchange for a project of individual utilitarian maximization and a world of competitive advantages. The undertaking largely surpassed previous attempts to make of Chile a laboratory of ideological experimentation."[5]

In this abridged summary, Juan Gabriel Valdes has shown how one country exemplifies the continuing centralized logic outlined in previous pages, to arrive today at General Pinochet's ideal, as stated by an early republican: "The executive power should exercise absolute control over the administration, without the legislative bodies doing anything but providing a few permanent laws, and meeting shortly, and with long recess periods in between those meetings. This is necessary in order to give vitality and respect to the executive."[6] From Christian Democrats, through Marxists, to military imposition of laissez-faire economics, a unitary norm has predominated. Now, what is one to expect with the news that the dictatorship has been overthrown?

It is not in Argentina's currently applauding masses, but in an incrementally changing political culture that one views the Latin America of tomorrow. As with Weber's capitalistic ethos, there is no reason to doubt that rational habits of democracy will be accepted when perceived by Everyman to be in his interest. It stretches credulity, however, to maintain that either the kind of democracy sought or the rational means thereto will duplicate our own. (It should be kept in mind that in terms of the human condition, Latin America's integration of individual, family, and religion into a meaningful whole is perhaps more natural and surely more satisfying than that of atomistic North Americans. Those cherished aspects of their existence are nearly all threatened by pluralistic premises.)

One of the most important events in Latin American history is in the making just across the Rio Grande. A centralized political party that has "won" every gubernatorial and presidential election since 1929, and dominated every office from "county sheriff" to the National Congress, is today being questioned by a growing opposition's demand for pluralist participation. The ambiguity of the situation lies in the fact that this opposition shares the same nonpluralist unitary tradition.

What will be the outcome? I know not, but in decisions such as these lies the future of Latin America.

Notes

One

1. Thomas O. Enders, speech to World Affairs Council in Washington, D.C., 16 July 1981; reported in *The New York Times*, 17 July 1981.
2. Thomas Aquinas, *De Regimine Principum*, Liber Primus, Caput. I.
3. *Ibid.*
4. Jaime Wheelock, "Nicaragua's Economy and the Fight Against Imperialism," in Tomas Borge, et al., *Sandinistas Speak* (New York: Pathfinder Press, 1982), 119.
5. *The Voice of Peron* (Buenos Aires: Subsecretaria de Informaciones de la Presidencia de la Nacion Argentina, 1950), 186.
6. Miguel Pombo, "Discurso Preliminar", *Constitucion de los Estados-Unidos de America*, Traducidas del Ingles al Espanol por el Ciudadano Miguel de Pombo (Bogota: En la Imprenta Patriotica de D. Nicolas Calvo, 1811), 73.
7. *Selected Writings of Bolivar*, Compiled by Vicente Lecuna, ed. Harold A. Bierck, Jr. (New York: The Colonial Press, 1951), 191-192.
8. *Constitution of the Republic of Guatemala*, 1965 (Washington, D.C., Pan American Union, 1966), Title II, Article 44.
9. In Mario Menendez Rodriguez, *Voices from El Salvador* (San Francisco: Solidarity Publications, 1983), 26.
10. *Selected Writings of Bolivar*, 22-23.
11. *Decretos del Libertador* (Caracas: Imprenta Nacional, 1961), Tomo I, 9.
12. From Laurence Birns, ed., *The End of Chilean Democracy* (New York: Seabury Continuum Book, 1973), 105, 109.

13. William Spence Robertson, *Rise of the Spanish-American Republics* (New York: Collier, 1961), 216.
14. *Selected Writings of Bolivar*, 191.
15. *Fidel Castro Speaks*, ed. Martin Kenner and James Petras (New York: Grove Press, 1969), 110.
16. Fidel Castro, *Cuba's Socialist Destiny* (New York: Fair Play for Cuba Committee, 1961), 7.
17. The figure usually given is 300,000 lives lost. See, for example, Harry Kantor, *Patterns of Politics and Political Systems in Latin America* (Chicago: Rand McNally, 1969), 400.
18. Jonathan Power, *Against Oblivion: Amnesty International's Fight for Human Rights* (London: Fontana, 1981), 107.
19. Jacobo Timerman, *Prisoner Without a Name, Cell Without a Number* (London: Penguin, 1982), 15.
20. Thomas Aquinas, *Ethics*, I, Commentary, lect. 2. Liberal democracy accepts the inalienability of rights because, unlike Latin America, no conflict between private interests and the undefined public good is seen to exist. Edwin S. Corwin synthesized this historical understanding: "That the public good might not always be compatible with the preservation of rights, and especially with the rights of property, never once occurs to him [Locke]. A century later the possibility did occur to Adam Smith, and was waived aside by his 'harmony of interests' theory." Edwin S. Corwin, *The "Higher Law" Background of American Constitutional Law* (Cornell University Press, Great Seal Books, 1959), 71.
21. "Constitution of the Republic of Honduras, 1982," *Constitutions of the World Series* (Dobbs Ferry, New York: Oceana Publications), Art. 77, 75, 78.
22. *Ibid.*, Title IV, Art. 38.
23. Lydia Chavez, "Trouble from Both Sides in El Salvador," *The New York Times*, 6 November 1983.
24. James McCartney, Knight-Ridder News Service, printed in Portland, Oregon, *Oregonian*, 2 December 1983.
25. *Selected Writings of Bolivar*, 188.
26. President Reagan's speech to Congress, as reported in *The Washington Spectator*, 1 August 1983, 3.
27. This discussion is lucidly summarized by Luis Maira, "The U.S. Debate on the Central American Crisis," in Richard R.

Fagan and Olga Pellicer, eds., *The Future of Central America* (Stanford, California: Stanford University Press, 1983). My quote is from pages 74-75.

28. *Ibid.*, 78ff.
29. *Ibid.*, 76.
30. *The National Bipartisan Commission on Central America Report* (10 January 1984), Chap. 8, 126.
31. Edelberto Torres-Rivas, "Seven Keys to Understanding the Central American Crisis," in Marlene Dixon and Susanne Jonas, eds., *Revolution and Intervention in Central America* (San Francisco: Synthesis Publications, 1983), revised ed., 164.
32. James Madison, *The Federalist,* #10.
33. *Selected Writings of Bolivar,* 183.
34. *Ibid.*, 21.
35. J. H. Plumb, *The Italian Renaissance* (New York: Harper Torchbooks, 1961), 20-21.
36. Junta Militar, "Edict No. 5," Sept. 1973; reprinted in Robert J. Alexander, *The Tragedy of Chile* (Westport, Conn: Greenwood Press, 1978), 453-454.
37. Niccolo Machiavelli, *The Prince*, Chap. 9.
38. Omar Torrijos, *La Batalla de Panama* (Buenos Aires: Editorial Universitaria de Buenos Aires, 1973), 71. Reflecting a culture-wide justification for "purifying" authority, Latin American caudillos, for example current generals Pinochet (Chile) and Stroessner (Paraguay), defend military coups as legitimate efforts to save their nations from totalitarianism. United States diplomats often stumble in dealing with these men because the illegitimacy of their roots appears to provide an *a fortiori* argument against their continued rule. But Latin leaders and subjects see it differently, blurring the distinction between elections and coups. Former Venezuelan dictator Marcos Perez Jimenez furnishes the more or less accepted rationale for at least temporary military intervention against an elected political order. "Totalitarianism does not come only from authoritarian regimes. At times it comes from the popular vote. It may be that a government has the purest origin, which is to say, that it has arisen through the popular vote, but in its actions it may evidence a totalitarian character."

Agustin Blanco Munoz, *Habla el General Marcos Perez Jimenez* (Caracas: Editorial Jose Marti, 1983), 109.

39. Niccolo Machiavelli, *The Prince*, Chap. 8.
40. *Commentary*, vol. 68, no. 5 (November 1979); 34-45.
41. Carlos Fuentes, "Harvard Commencement Speech," 1983. *Congressional Record*, vol. 129, no. 99 (July 15, 1983).
42. Niccolo Machiavelli, *The Prince*, Chap. 20. "The best fortress is to be found in the love of the people, for although you may have fortresses they will not save you if you are hated by the people."
43. Speech on election in El Salvador, 1 March 1984, *Department of State* Bulletin (April 1984); 77.

Two

1. Jeane Kirkpatrick, *U.S. News and World Report*, 2 March 1981, 49-50.
2. George F. Kennan, in Martin F. Herz, ed., *Decline of the West* (Georgetown University, 1978), 18.
3. Hannah Arendt, *On Revolution* (Viking, 1963), 90.
4. Nicolas Berdyaev, *The Origin of Russian Communism* (University of Michigan, 1960), 139; 113.
5. Hans J. Morgenthau, *The Restoration of American Politics* (University of Chicago, 1962), 239.
6. Arendt, *On Revolution*, 108.
7. Meaningful discussion between the Sandinistas and *Contras* could happen if the two sides decided to take President Reagan at his word. To the extent the U.S. has a stated policy toward Nicaragua it is to see the Sandinistas and *Contras* reach a bi-lateral settlement; the unstated tri-lateral agenda calls for a negotiated end to Sandinista dominion. So far the Sandinistas have resisted direct talks in order to avoid legitimizing the *Contras* as a force independent of U.S. imperialism. Should that position change and both parties begin to converse as independents, this administration's bluff might indeed be called.

   The ancient Greeks warned, never petition the Gods in jest, lest they reward you in earnest. Any conceivable agreement that might emerge out of a truly bi-lateral accord would inherently mean recognition by U.S. proxies of the Marxist/ nationalist government in Managua—what the Reagan administration has spent so much materiel and so many Nicaraguan lives to prevent.

8. Barrington Moore, Jr., *Reflections on the Causes of Human Misery* (Boston: Beacon Press, 1972), Chap. 1.
9. Plato, *The Republic*, Part IV, Bk. VIII.
10. *The New York Times*, 3 September 1985.
11. John Locke, *The Second Treatise on Civil Government*, Chap. V, par. 49; Chap. II, par. 5; Chap. V, par. 34; Chap. II, par. 6.
12. From Robert McAfee Brown, *Unexpected News: Reading the Bible with Third World Eyes* (Philadelphia: Westminster Press, 1984), 93.
13. Locke, *Second Treatise*, Chap. II, par. 6.
14. Shirley Christian, "Nicaragua," in *New York Times Book Review*, 28 July 1985. Right-wing populist authoritarian leaders agree that liberal values and electoral events should take second place to social welfare. For example, former Venezuelan strongman Marcos Perez Jimenez acknowledged the supreme importance of "the plurality of command, the freedom of expression, etc." under democratic governments. During his regime (1948-1958), however, "these things, yes, had importance, but were not the essentials of the moment. That which one had to do was to eradicate paludism, the syphilis that was killing the Venezuelan population, to endow the country with adequate lines of communication, eradicate the poor housing that existed then and achieve those things that directly affected the condition of individuals. . . . Peoples filled with epidemics do not become outstanding individuals in the human community. The first thing one had to do, consequently, was to provide security for the people in order to form them justly, to give them adequate cultural levels. Not everything can be reduced to liberty of expression. And I think all that is very good, but first one had to feed, house and educate the people in order that they come to understand the full significance of liberty." Agustin Blanco Munoz, *Habla el General Marcos Perez Jimenez* (Caracas: Editorial Jose Marti, 1983), 30.

15. Alexis de Tocqueville, *The Old Regime*, Part III, Chap. 3.
16. Juan M. del Aguila, *Cuba: Dilemmas of a Revolution* (Boulder, Colorado: Westview Press, 1984), 1.
17. Nothing in this essay is meant to hint that the totalitarian Left furnishes an alternate "school" for Central America. When the Russians put down the Hungarian Revolution (1958) and instituted "a reign of terror that has as much right to be called socialist as the executioners of the Inquisition had to be called Christians," Albert Camus wrote: "Contemptuous teachers, unaware that they were thereby insulting the working classes, had assured us that the masses could readily get along without liberty if only they were given bread." Albert Camus, *Resistance, Rebellion, and Death* (New York: Modern Library, 1960), 118-119.
18. James LeMoyne, *The New York Times*, 3 August 1985, quoting "a foreign diplomat."
19. *The New York Times*, 29 July 1985.
20. Tomas Borge, in *Sandinistas Speak* (New York: Pathfinder Press, 1982), 102.
21. *The New York Times*, 1 December 1985.
22. Arendt, *On Revolution*, 87.
23. Thucydides, *History of the Peloponnesian War*, Bk. III, par. 46.
24. Madison, *The Federalist*, #10.
25. William Graham Sumner, *The Conquest of the United States by Spain* (Lake Bluff, Illinois: Henry Regnery, n.d.), 146.

Three

1. Thucydides, *History*, Bk. III, par. 45.
2. Elliott Abrams, *The New York Times*, 13 January 1986.
3. *The National Bipartisan Commission on Central America Report*, 127.
4. President Reagan, Speech, 1 March 1985.
5. President Reagan, reported in Salem, Oregon, *Statesman*, 16 April 1985.
6. Portland, Oregon, *Oregonian*, 23 February 1985.
7. Jean Calvin, *On God and Political Duty* (New York: Bobbs - Merrill, 1956), 5.

8. Kennan's formulation read: "Soviet pressure against the free institutions of the Western world is something that can be contained by the adroit and vigilant application of counter-force at a series of constantly shifting geographical and political points, corresponding to the shifts and maneuvers of Soviet policy." George F. Kennan, *American Diplomacy*, 1900-1950 (New York: Mentor, 1951), 99.

9. John Dillenberger, ed., *Martin Luther: Selections from His Writings* (New York: Doubleday Anchor, 1961), 398.

10. Rigoberta Menchu, in Jonathan L. Fried, ed., *Guatemala in Rebellion* (New York: Grove Press, 1983), 199.

11. From Mariano Picon-Salas, *A Cultural History of Spanish America* (Berkeley, California: University of California Press, 1963), 20.

12. Lewis Hanke, *Aristotle and the American Indians* (Lake Bluff, Illinois: Henry Regnery, 1959), 26.

13. *Oregonian*, 24 February 1985, B1.

14. McKinley, in Samuel Flagg Bemis, *A Diplomatic History of the United States*, 4th ed. (New York: Holt, 1955), 472.

15. Milton Eisenhower, *Report to the President: United States-Latin American Relations* (Department of State, Inter-American Series 55, January 1959), 16.

16. Hanke, *Aristotle*, 86.

17. Perry Miller, *Errand into the Wilderness* (Belknap Press, 1956).

18. Jean Jacques Rousseau, *The Social Contract*, Bk. I, Chap. V.

19. *Psychological Operations in Guerrilla Warfare* (New York: Vintage Books, 1985), 56. This "democratic ends justify repressive means" attitude is not unique to the current administration. President Harry Truman in September 1950 approved *NSC 68: United States Objectives and Programs for National Security* which established our early Cold War policy. According to that document, "in relations between nations, the prime reliance of the free society is on the strength and appeal of its idea, and it feels no compulsion sooner or later to bring all societies into conformity with it." The democratic way is harder than the authoritarian way, states *NSC 68*, in that under the former the individual must exercise discrimination, "that while pursuing through free inquiry the search for

truth he knows when he should commit an act of faith; that he distinguish between the necessity for tolerance and the necessity for just suppression." From Thomas H. Etzold and John Lewis Gaddis, eds., *Containment: Documents on American Policy and Strategy*, 1945-1950 (New York: Columbia University Press, 1978), 388, 403.

20. Rousseau, *Social Contract*, Bk. I, Chap. V.
21. Thucydides, *History*, Bk. III, par. 37.
22. Aristotle's distinction is found in *The Politics*, Bk. III, Chap. VI.
23. Thucydides, *History*, Bk. III, par. 82.
24. Thucydides, *History*, Bk. V, par. 90.
25. From Edward J. Williams, *The Political Themes of Inter-American Relations* (North Scituate, Massachusetts: Duxbury Press, 1971), 5.
26. Juan Jose Arevalo, *The Shark and the Sardines* (Secaucus, New Jersey: Lyle Stuart, 1961).
27. R. R. Palmer, *A History of the Modern World* (New York: Knopf, 1956), 121ff.

Afterword

1. See author's "The Tradition of Monistic Democracy in Latin America," *Journal of the History of Ideas* (August 1974).
2. Carl Huneeus Madge, *Los Chilenos y la Politica* (Santiago: Centro de Estudios de la Realidad Contemporanea, 1987).
3. From *Democracia en Chile: Doce Conferencias* (Santiago: Corporacion de Investigaciones Economicas para Latinoamerica, 1986), 182-183. Also see Jose Joaquin Brunner, "Cultura y politica en la lucha por la democracia," in *Siete Ensayos Sobre Democracia y Socialismo en Chile* (Santiago: Ediciones Documentas, 1986).
4. *Ibid.*, 183-184.
5. *Ibid.*, 185.
6. Juan Egana, *Ocios Filosoficos y Poeticos en la Quinta de las Delicias* (Londres: Impreso por D. Manuel Calero, 1829), 69. Presently Chile has no Congress. General Pinochet has slyly hinted that when it next convenes the legislature should meet somewhere on the coast.